Apple Training Series

Xsan 2 Administration

A Guide to Designing, Deploying, and Maintaining Xsan

Robert Kite, Ph.D., et al.

Apple Training Series: Xsan 2 Administration
Robert Kite, Ph.D., et al.
Copyright © 2009 by Apple, Inc.

Published by Peachpit Press. For information on Peachpit Press books, contact:

Peachpit Press
1249 Eighth Street
Berkeley, CA 94710
(510) 524-2178
www.peachpit.com

To report errors, please send a note to errata@peachpit.com.
Peachpit Press is a division of Pearson Education.

Apple Series Editor: Serena Herr
Editor: Bob Lindstrom
Contributing Writers: David Long, Jeremy Roush
Technical Editor: Brendan Boykin
Copy Editor: Elissa Rabellino
Production Coordinator: Danielle Foster
Compositor: Danielle Foster
Indexer: Jack Lewis
Cover Illustrator: Mimi Heft

ISBN-13: 978-0-321-61322-6
ISBN 10: 0-321-61322-8

9 8 7 6 5 4 3 2 1

Printed and bound in the United States of America

Acknowledgments

A project like this you finish only with the help of friends, colleagues, and family.

Thanks to my family—Darcy, Kelly, Alex, and Kate—for putting up with me during the weeks of sleep deprivation.

Ravi, Arek Dreyer, Rick Wylie, and David Long provided invaluable insight, knowledge, and help.

Apple cohorts Adam Green, Eryk Vershen, John Wolfe, Andrew Johnson, Joe Schuepbach, Aric Marshall, Doug Brooks, and Shane Ross gave us the *real* answers when we needed them most.

The engineers at techIT Solutions—Allan Sanderson, James "Tip" Lovingood, Danielle James, and Chris Angerame—proved that sometimes field experience is all you need. Tip, thanks for running the lab and doing so much testing.

Vincent Louque, Kealoha Yoshioka, Chris Niemietz, and the team from the Product Placement Group made important contributions.

Thanks to our edit team: Serena Herr for all the pushing, Bob Lindstrom for an amazing edit, and Brendan Boykin for the reality check, suggestions, and guidance.

And lastly, LeRoy Dennison. You did this to me and I won't forget it. Thanks for the opportunity.

Contents at a Glance

Table of Contents

Getting Started

Welcome to the official training reference for Xsan 2, Apple's enterprise-class SAN file system and management software.

This book serves as a self-paced guide and reference, and is designed to help you build the basic skills you need to design, deploy, and support an Xsan 2 installation. It is based on the premise that a training book should go beyond a basic tour of Xsan installations by providing you with a solid understanding of the technologies underlying network storage systems, along with practical, effective techniques that you will use on a daily basis when implementing and administering an Xsan solution in a professional setting.

This book is also part of the courseware for the Apple Certified Xsan 2 Administrator training course and serves as a preparation for the Apple Certified Xsan 2 Administrator exam.

The Methodology

Apple Training Series books emphasize hands-on training. The exercises in this book are designed so that you can explore and learn the tools necessary to deploy and manage an Xsan 2 solution.

This book serves as a thorough introduction and guide to Xsan 2, and is not meant to be a sole, definitive reference. Because Xsan is an extremely flexible and scalable storage area network solution, there will be unique and advanced implementations of the solution that require more individual attention than any reference book could provide.

For most Xsan implementations, however, this book offers structured, step-by-step instruction covering what you need to know to design, deploy, and administer a professional Xsan 2 installation.

Course Structure

The chapters move along in a predictable fashion, starting with the basic concepts and technologies that underlie storage area networking and the Xsan file system, moving on to planning and deploying an Xsan, and finishing up with a thorough discussion of client management, volume management, and Xsan maintenance and troubleshooting.

Chapter 1   Basic concepts of storage area networks

Chapter 2   Planning an Xsan solution

Chapter 3   Deploying an Xsan solution

Chapter 4   Managing clients

Chapter 5   Managing volumes

Chapter 6   Maintaining and troubleshooting

If you already have an Xsan installation deployed, you can simply skip ahead to the chapters that deal with management, maintenance, and troubleshooting.

System Requirements

This book assumes a basic knowledge of the Macintosh operating environment and storage networks in general. Here's the minimum you need to complete the lessons in this book:

▶   Volumes of shared storage, stored on an Apple Xserve RAID or Promise VTrak RAID.

▶   Underlying Fibre Channel and Ethernet networks

▶   An Xsan file system

▶   One computer acting as a metadata controller

▶   At least two computers acting as client computers

Certification

Apple Training Series: Xsan 2 Administration provides a thorough preparation for the Apple Certified Xsan 2 Administrator exam, offered by Apple Inc.

Before you take the exam, you should review the lessons and ideas in this book. Each chapter ends with a summary, called "What You've Learned," of the main ideas in the chapter, along with useful review questions and answers that you can use as a self-quiz.

You should also download and review the Skills Assessment Guide, which lists the exam objectives, the score required to pass the exam, and how to register for it. To download the Skills Assessment Guide, visit http://train.apple.com/certification.

Earning Apple technical certification shows employers that you have achieved a high level of technical proficiency with Apple productions. You'll also join a growing community of skilled professionals who share Apple certification.

For more information on Apple certification, visit http://train.apple.com/certification.

About the Apple Training Series

Apple Training Series: Xsan 2 Administration is part of the official training series for Apple products, which was developed by experts in the field and certified by Apple Inc. The lessons are designed to let you learn at your own pace.

For those who prefer to learn in an instructor-led setting, Apple also offers training courses at Apple Authorized Training Centers worldwide. These courses, which use the Apple Training Series books as their curriculum, are taught by Apple Certified Trainers and balance concepts and lectures with hands-on labs and exercises. Apple Authorized Training Centers have been carefully selected and have met Apple's highest standards in all areas, including facilities, instructors, course delivery, and infrastructure. The goal of the program is to offer Apple customers, from beginners to the most seasoned professionals, the highest quality training experience.

To find an Authorized Training Center near you, go to www.apple.com/training.

1

Time   This chapter takes approximately 90 minutes to complete.

Goals   Understand the three main networked storage architectures

Describe the benefits, components, and underlying technology of storage networking

Define a cluster file system and describe how it takes advantage of SAN storage architecture

Recognize the benefits and key features of a SAN, including its components and their distinguishing characteristics

Describe the underlying technology required for Fibre Channel to function in a SAN environment

Understand the importance of dedicating an Ethernet network solely to SAN traffic

Gain an understanding of the Xsan-specific implementation of a SAN

Describe the basic structure of an Xsan volume and the Xsan file system

Identify the key features of Xsan 2

Chapter 1

Concepts: Understanding Storage Area Networks

The goal of this book is to teach you how to design, implement, and support an Xsan 2 installation. But before you start, it's important to understand the technologies that make up the solution and to see where Xsan fits in the range of solutions for shared storage. The best place to begin is with an overview of the storage networking space.

Storage networking—the practice of maintaining a high-speed subnetwork whose primary purpose is the transfer of data among storage devices and computer systems—has many benefits, and you can implement storage networking in different ways to take advantage of those benefits. Xsan, for example, is a cluster file system that leverages the benefits of Fibre Channel storage networking.

In this chapter, you'll look at the foundational concepts of storage networking, focusing primarily on SAN (Storage Area Network) architectures and related Fibre Channel and cluster file system technologies. In the second half of the chapter, you'll concentrate on Apple's Xsan solution and explain how it benefits users who need high-performance access to a shared pool of storage.

After mastering this chapter, you should be able to describe how a SAN works and what benefits are obtained by using Xsan as your file system. You'll be able to describe and identify the various components required to build a SAN, as well as the key features of Xsan 2 and storage area networks in general.

Storage Networking Architectures

Virtually every industry is experiencing exponential growth in storage requirements. Beyond demand for capacity, organizations are increasingly concerned with data protection, and face increasing demand for near-instant and reliable access to mission-critical files.

To address these needs, three basic types of storage networking architectures have emerged: direct-attached storage (DAS), network-attached storage (NAS), and the storage area network (SAN). All three aim to serve the same basic purpose: to securely store large amounts of data while making it instantly available in an efficient, predictable, and flexible way to a large number of simultaneous users.

To appreciate the benefits of Xsan, it's helpful to understand the differences among storage architectures and the advantages of a SAN file system.

Direct-Attached Storage (DAS)

In a DAS configuration, disk drives or storage systems are connected directly to a server via SCSI or Fibre Channel.

The host server formats the DAS using a compatible disk file system—such as the Unix file system (UFS) or hierarchical file system (HFS+). The server shares the storage with clients over a local Ethernet network, using a network file system protocol such as AFP, SMB/CIFS, or NFS.

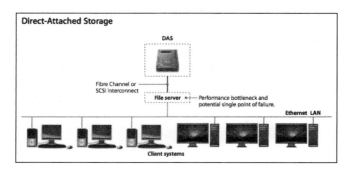

DAS configurations using RAID storage devices are often used in film and television workflows during video ingest and output—workflows that require very high data throughput and storage capacity. Workstations can then share this material over an Ethernet LAN, but not at the speeds necessary for real-time playback.

DAS is the simplest storage solution to configure and use, but the throughput loss incurred when sharing the DAS over Ethernet, as well as the performance bottleneck (and potential point of failure) of the single file server, makes it unsuitable for many workflows.

Network-Attached Storage (NAS)

The centerpiece of a NAS architecture is a *NAS appliance*: a storage device with a built-in file server and Ethernet ports. This NAS appliance connects to a local area network and, like a DAS solution, shares storage with clients over Ethernet using a network file system. A NAS appliance typically uses a specialized server operating system that's designed to make it easier to set up and maintain file sharing than when using a general-purpose server.

NAS solutions can work well for small workgroups without high capacity or throughput demands, but they have the same single-server performance bottleneck as a DAS solution, and can also be difficult to scale as storage demands increase.

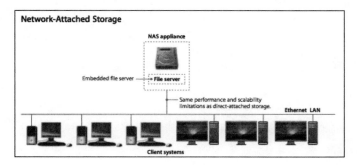

Limitations of DAS and NAS Solutions

DAS and NAS architectures suffer from the same limitations, including:

► **Single point of failure.** The DAS host or NAS appliance is the single point of access to storage—and, potentially, a single point of failure.

▶ **Performance bottlenecks.** Since all file system requests must go through a single workstation or server, performance bottlenecks occur. The performance hit can be magnified by Ethernet bandwidth limitations.

▶ **Difficult scalability.** In both solutions, scalability is limited by the number of storage devices that can be attached to the server. It's also cumbersome to add disks or RAID arrays to DAS or NAS systems.

Storage Area Network (SAN)

A storage area network, or SAN, is a method of aggregating storage devices into a single "virtual" storage volume and allowing multiple servers and client computers to access that volume simultaneously over a dedicated high-speed network.

To the servers and workstations, the virtual volume looks just like a DAS device— like a big hard drive. The difference is that, with a SAN file system such as Xsan, all the servers are connected to the volume via a Fibre Channel switch and can access the storage volume at the same time. These host servers can then share the data with additional clients on the local Ethernet network using a network file system protocol such as AFP, SMB/CIFS, or NFS.

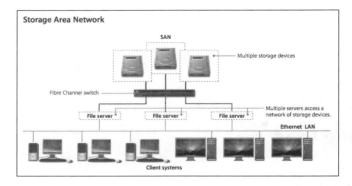

Benefits of Storage Area Networking

A SAN requires more planning than DAS and NAS solutions, but offers superior through-put, capacity, and scalability. Workflows that require very high bandwidth data transfer and high storage capacity at the workstation level gain both. Let's take a moment to look at the benefits of SAN architectures in detail.

High-Performance, Concurrent File Sharing

Unlike NAS or DAS systems—which use network file-sharing protocols to deliver stored data to clients—a SAN typically uses a high-speed Fibre Channel interconnect, or *switch*. SCSI data and commands are sent across the SAN over Fibre Channel protocols, which allows faster file access and more efficient sharing. This enables many users in a workflow to work with the same data at the same time, facilitating collaboration and increasing productivity.

Network-Based Storage Management

By consolidating data onto one shared virtual volume, you can use all available storage resources more efficiently and with greater flexibility. Storage devices can be connected through a Fibre Channel switch to any computer or server on the SAN. Centralized stor-age also streamlines management and makes it easier to control user access.

Eliminating Single Points of Failure

Because a SAN file system gives multiple servers access to shared storage, you can elimi-nate single points of failure. For example, if one server fails, another server can seamlessly take over its job and continue to serve the data to clients on the network.

Flexible SAN Topology

With a SAN file system, it's easy to add capacity as storage needs grow. Simply connect more RAID devices to expand the capacity of existing SAN volumes, or to create new vol-umes that can be shared among the attached servers.

To increase the available bandwidth or processing power of your network services, you can add more servers running the Xsan file system. These new servers can have immediate block-level access to the SAN storage volumes and can be used to host network services such as web serving, file sharing, or media streaming for additional network or Internet clients.

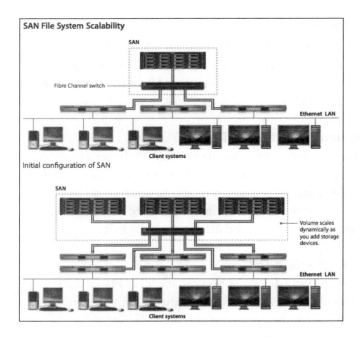

The Benefits of Consolidated Storage

In summary, a SAN file system provides important benefits over DAS and NAS architectures:

▶ Fast, concurrent file sharing for streamlined workflows

▶ Increased uptime by eliminating single points of failure

▶ Simplified administration and access controls using directory-based management

▶ Reduced costs through more efficient disk use.

▶ Flexible deployment and easy scalability without interrupting operations

Why a SAN File System?

A SAN by itself—without a SAN file system—must assign, or *provision*, each LUN to an individual server or computer for its exclusive use. This effectively separates data into *silos*, stopping short of the collaboration benefits of a SAN, as well as many of the management and scalability benefits.

Why Use a Cluster File System?

A *cluster file system* is a distributed file system that essentially manages a cluster of servers (rather than just one server) so that they all work together to deliver files to client computers. To the clients, the cluster is transparent—it's just the storage volume—and the file system software deals behind the scenes with distributing requests to elements of the storage cluster.

Without a cluster file system like Xsan, the SAN storage has to be dedicated to individual hosts for their exclusive use, in a manner similar to using direct-attached storage— although it's still more manageable and efficient. Here's how it works:

Storage devices on a SAN appear as logical unit numbers (LUNs). A LUN may be a disk, a V-Trak RAID, or a slice of a RAID set—think of it as a virtual volume of storage. Xserve RAID and Promise storage can be configured into many LUNs. For example, the illustration below shows three LUNs.

A SAN by itself—without a SAN file system—must assign, or *provision*, each LUN to an individual server or computer for its exclusive use. This involves something called *LUN mapping*, which you'll explore later. After one or more LUNs are provisioned to a computer, the computer initializes the LUNs with a disk file system, such as HFS+ or UFS. As a result, data stored on LUN A is only available to server A and to those network clients attached to Server A. It's the same for LUNs and servers B and C.

The result is that data is separated in *silos*, accessible only through a specific server. This effectively eliminates the collaborative benefits of a SAN, as well as many of the management and scalability benefits.

With a cluster file system like Xsan, however, the file system can simplify or eliminate the provisioning process. In the architectural comparison below, all of the LUNs are aggregated into a single volume. Again, the volume looks just like direct-attached storage to the servers (like a big hard drive). The difference is that all the servers can access this volume, enabling simultaneous access to the same data from multiple systems.

By combining the data into a single shared volume, you get much more flexibility, allowing you to use all available storage resources more efficiently.

Because all the hosts have access to the volume, you also eliminate any single point of failure for accessing the volume. For example, if one of the servers fails, another server can take over its job and continue to serve the data to clients on the network.

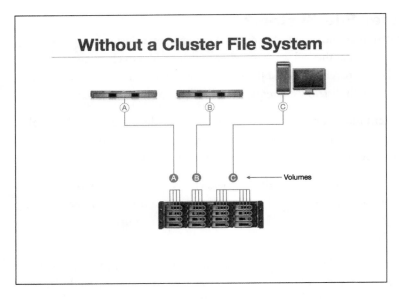

To summarize, with a SAN cluster file system:

▶   LUN provisioning is reduced and data silos are eliminated.

▶   The volumes are shared.

▶   Storage is used more efficiently.

▶   Storage management is easier.

In a standard SAN, the host manages the file system—just as with DAS. However, the storage devices are separated from the host, allowing storage resources and computing resources to scale independently. The clients access the storage through the server file system.

With a cluster file system, the host manages the client requests, but the SAN file system manages the storage for all the hosts. The hosts become clients to the file system. SAN bandwidth, file sharing, efficient allocation of storage resources, and centralized management become features of the entire SAN, not just of each host on the SAN.

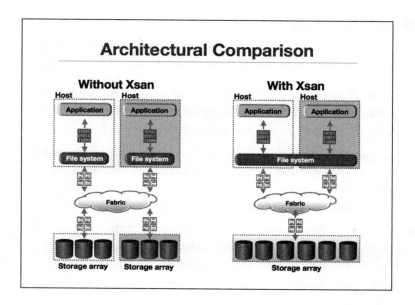

Understanding Fibre Channel

Fibre Channel is a set of advanced data-transport standards that allow large amounts of data to be moved reliably, at multi-gigabit speeds, between computers, servers, disk arrays, and other devices. Traditional data-network technologies—such as Ethernet—are designed for chaotic, distributed environments. They support many devices and long distances, but data delivery can be slow or inconsistent. Fibre Channel combines the best of both worlds. It supports many devices and longer distances, and it provides reliable data delivery.

Although technologies other than Fibre Channel have been used—and continue to be used—to build SANs, most SANs today are built on Fibre Channel.

In this section, we take a look at how Fibre Channel works, the benefits it offers, and how it compares with other protocols and network solutions.

> **NOTE ▶** This section is intended as a Fibre Channel reference and goes into the topic in some depth. For now, treat it as an overview of Fibre Channel, and rest assured that you will see many of these concepts again in later chapters, as you learn how to plan and deploy an Xsan.

Why Use Fibre Channel for Xsan?

Apple chose Fibre Channel for high-end storage connectivity because of three main benefits: its high bandwidth, its proven reliability, and its guaranteed in-order delivery of data packets.

▶ **High speed.** In its current generation, Fibre Channel provides consistent bandwidth in the range of 4 gigabits per second. This rate is expected to double within a few years to 8 Gbit/s, keeping up with the foreseeable needs of network users.

▶ **Proven reliability.** Fibre Channel was initially embraced by virtually all of the world's banks, Fortune 500 companies, and other institutions that required reliable, on-time data delivery at any cost. Today this same mission-critical data center reliability is available to any business or organization at much lower cost.

▶ **Guaranteed in-order delivery.** Fibre Channel guarantees in-order delivery of raw block data, which greatly boosts network efficiency and is required by applications such as video streaming. Fibre Channel naturally streams video frames in order, eliminating reassembly bottlenecks that would otherwise noticeably delay the video's required frames-per-second play speed.

Fibre Channel Terminology

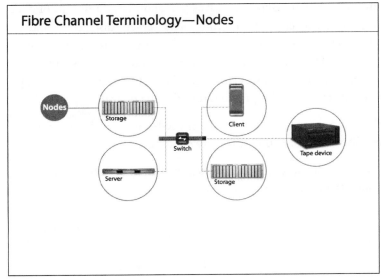

Nodes

Devices connected to a Fibre Channel network—such as workstations, servers, and RAIDs—are called *nodes*. Nodes present the data to the Fibre Channel network. They operate at a higher level than the Fibre Channel physical layer, and they do not know whether they are attached to a SCSI bus or a Fibre Channel infrastructure.

Interconnects

Switches and hubs are not nodes, but interconnect devices through which the data passes. Interconnect devices are transparent to the nodes.

Initiators and Targets

Hosts such as servers and workstations, which send SCSI commands over the network, are known as *initiators*. Storage devices such as the Promise RAID and Xserve RAIDs, which wait for and respond to initiator commands, are known as *targets*.

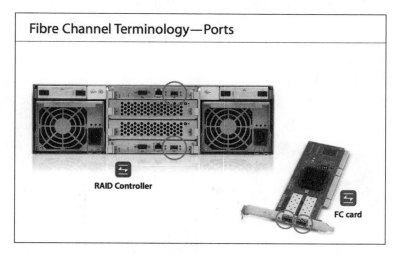

Fibre Channel Terminology—Ports

RAID Controller

FC card

Ports

Each node has at least one access point, or port, and Fibre Channel switches have many ports. In Fibre Channel terminology, ports are more than just physical interfaces. They are intelligent interfaces to the Fibre Channel network, and as such they perform important functions.

▶ Ports are the nodes' interface to the Fibre Channel network.

▶ Ports transmit and receive data to and from the network.

► Ports are responsible for actively controlling and managing Fibre Channel operations, such as fabric initialization and loop initialization.

► The World Wide Name (WWN) is a unique identifier embedded into the port or node during the manufacturing process. The WWN is usually referred to as the WWPN, as this is the name used to connect to the switch.

► The World Wide Port Name (WWPN) is a unique identifier for each port and is used when connecting to a switch. To view the WWPN for a Fibre Channel card, use the Fibre Channel preference pane in System Preferences. Note that Apple Fibre Channel cards have a unique WWPN for each port on the card.

► The World Wide Node Name (WWNN) is used to uniquely identify a device and is used mainly for dual-pathing software. To view the WWPN for a Fibre Channel card, use the Fibre Channel preference pane in System Preferences. Note that Apple Fibre Channel cards have a unique WWNN for each port on the card.

► Fibre Channel ID (FCID) is a dynamically assigned Layer 2 address.

Links

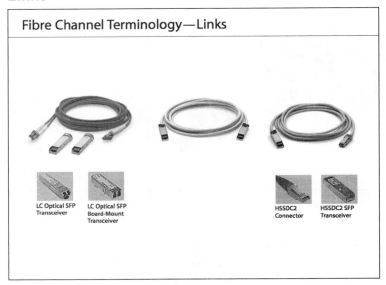

Fibre Channel Terminology—Links

LC Optical SFP
Transceiver

LC Optical SFP
Board-Mount
Transceiver

HSSDC2
Connector

HSSDC2 SFP
Transceiver

Ports are physically connected to one another using links. A link consists of all the hardware needed to make the connection, including cables, connectors, and optical-electrical transceivers. Fibre Channel links carry Fibre Channel transmissions from the transmitting port to the receiving port.

Fibre Channel and Protocols

Ethernet, SCSI, and other older input/output protocols were typically constructed with specific rules, or sets of commands, governing server-to-server and server-to-storage system communications. Such I/O protocols dictate how the physical interface should look, giving rise to a profusion of cables and connectors.

Fibre Channel designers took a different approach. Segregating the functions of data transport from the functions that impart the meaning of the data, they fashioned Fibre Channel not just as a protocol, but as a carrier of protocols—including SCSI-3 and IP command sets.

Like other network protocols such as Ethernet and IP, Fibre Channel is designed in a layered model. Each layer has a specific function that it performs on the data as it passes between the application and the operating system, the Fibre Channel network, and the storage devices.

Fibre Channel operates at the lower levels of the networking stack, and, generally speaking, it is a link-level protocol. For communicating with storage, the SCSI-3 command set is used on top of the Fibre Channel transport.

The term *SCSI* is used to refer to either a type of cabling or a set of commands used to talk to storage devices. Starting with SCSI-3, the cable definition was separated from the command set. So, while Fibre Channel can be described as a replacement for SCSI cabling technology, it is also true that Fibre Channel still uses SCSI commands.

Because of its SCSI heritage, Fibre Channel inherits the terms *target* and *initiator*. A target is a device on a Fibre Channel network that receives SCSI I/O commands, and an initiator is a device that issues SCSI I/O commands. On a simple SAN, you can think of targets as the storage devices (such as a Promise RAID), and initiators as the computer nodes on the SAN.

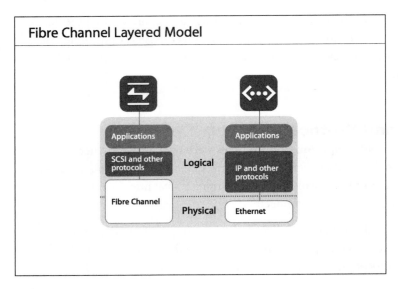

One benefit of this design is ready compatibility. No established command set needs to be re-created from scratch to work on a Fibre Channel network. Another benefit is that multiple protocols can be in use simultaneously, boosting network performance.

Comparing Protocols

In a storage environment, there are performance, cost, and future-growth implications to consider when comparing data-transfer protocols. Ethernet-based direct-attached and network-attached storage each have their own best-suited applications and specific limitations, but for transferring block data, Fibre Channel is the leading protocol choice for a number of reasons.

Fibre Channel and Ethernet

Ethernet's low cost and relatively easy setup make it one of the most common network protocols. It often provides the local area network connection between clients and servers, including SAN servers, and in this role, it works well.

As a protocol, however, Ethernet is not designed for transferring block data in a networked storage environment. The problem lies in the way that Ethernet handles data collisions—the errors that result when multiple computers try to transmit data simultaneously on the same network. As network usage increases, the number of collisions in an Ethernet network can grow dramatically, eventually consuming all available bandwidth.

In contrast, the asynchronous protocol design of Fibre Channel ensures that even when network loading is heavy, collisions are handled efficiently, maintaining maximum throughput.

Fibre Channel and iSCSI

iSCSI is one of the most talked-about new storage delivery protocols. Very few large-scale iSCSI deployments exist, so it has yet to be "data center hardened."

iSCSI proponents claim that it is less expensive to implement than Fibre Channel; but with Apple and other vendors driving down Fibre Channel prices, any cost advantage is eroding. iSCSI is asynchronous, as is Fibre Channel, and built on an underlying TCP/IP protocol, which is broadly supported and well understood by the IT community. However, TCP/IP saddles iSCSI with a software-centric orientation that doesn't always work to its advantage. Because the iSCSI command set has been implemented only in server-based software, it incurs significant processing overhead.

In contrast, the Fibre Channel command set was encoded in silicon early in the protocol's development, making it much more efficient than iSCSI at any level of processing power and more suitable for the data-transfer loading of a networked storage environment.

Fibre Channel and Infiniband

Infiniband is a new storage delivery protocol that uses its own, channel-based approach to distribute I/O processing. It is a transport network that can support iSCSI and Fibre Channel protocols.

Like Fibre Channel and iSCSI, Infiniband is both asynchronous and switched fabric. Participating nodes can be concurrently interconnected rather than having to share media (as does Ethernet) or having to share bandwidth (as does Token Ring).

Infiniband is still a new technology. Its visibility is mainly limited to research computing, and it is likely to be some time before Infiniband gains broad use in storage network environments.

Fibre Channel and IP

Like IP, Fibre Channel has a burned-in identifier for each node or device. In IP networking, this is usually the MAC address; in Fibre Channel it's the World Wide Name (WWN).

Both Fibre Channel and IP are routable. Fibre Channel makes no distinction between switching and routing.

Names in Fibre Channel are fixed; in IP they can be configured. As with IP, an ID can be dynamically assigned. In IP, this would be the IP address. In Fibre Channel, this would be the Fibre Channel ID. A Fibre Channel ID is resolved to a WWN by the Fibre Channel switch. In IP, a host name is resolved to an IP address via a DNS server.

Fibre Channel versus IP

Fibre Channel	IP
Dynamic Layer 2 address (FCID)	Fixed address (MAC)
	Dynamic address (IP)
Routable	Routable
Names are fixed (WWN)	Names are configurable
Switch name server resolves name to Fibre Channel Port ID (FCID)	DNS resolves name to IP
	ARP resolves IP to MAC

How Fibre Channel Works with Networks

Though it has many features of a network, Fibre Channel is less a network than a high-speed switching system that interconnects relatively local drives. With its high bandwidth and ability to support multiple protocols simultaneously, Fibre Channel enables near-instant access to massive amounts of data in SANs and other computing environments.

A *channel* (as in Fibre *Channel*) is a directly attached and well-structured mechanism designed to transmit data between a host and a small number of devices in a known configuration. Channels generally use a parallel architecture that can support high speeds, but only over short distances.

Because channels are static and well structured, data can be routed between devices with minimal delays, providing low latency. Channels perform only minimal decision-making tasks, and these tasks are performed by hardware, ensuring a minimal load on the host's CPU.

Networks are designed to dynamically adjust to environments in which the number and configuration of devices is expected to change. Because networks route data through complex and changing paths, end-to-end latency can be significantly higher than in a channel. Networks generally use a serial architecture, which supports high speeds and long distances.

In a network, more decision-making tasks must be performed on the fly in order to route data. These tasks are performed mainly by software running on each host, consuming CPU cycles and slowing data delivery. In a typical IP host, the entire TCP/IP networking stack is in software—usually in the operating system of the host device. In a Fibre Channel network, the network stack is significantly embedded in hardware in the form of the Host Bus Adapter.

Channels and Networks

I/O Channel (e.g., SCSI bus)	Network (e.g., Ethernet)
Few devices	Many devices
Static addressing	Dynamic addressing
Low latency	High latency
Short distances	Long distances
Hardware-based delivery management	Software-based delivery management

Network Limits and Characteristics

Collision-based Ethernet networks are ubiquitous largely because they allow multiple clients to share retrieved data in a very simple and economical way. Such networks succeed when supporting front-end functions but are too inefficient for block-level storage environments, such as those found in data centers or video installations.

For throughput, scalability, and attainable network lengths, Fibre Channel is far superior to Ethernet.

▶ **Data throughput.** With the currently available 4 gigabit Fibre Channel in the network, data transfer rates are close to 400 MB/s. In a Gigabit Ethernet network, however, collision management claims so much bandwidth that even 1 Gb rates are difficult to achieve consistently.

▶ **Scalability.** Whether it supports a single point-to-point link or hundreds of integrated enterprise servers, a Fibre Channel network performs with equal reliability, high rates, and flexible configuration. It achieves scalable densities up to thousands of ports. Although IP-based storage networks theoretically can scale to hundreds of ports, there is no widespread use to demonstrate this capability.

▶ **Network lengths.** Fibre Channel's physical media—the switches and cables that carry the data—can be either copper or optical. Performance is the same, though copper must be limited in length to less than 3 meters. In comparison, standard Ethernet networks are copper based and use twisted-pair cabling. Without the benefit of repeaters, long-haul copper Ethernet networks are limited to 100 to 200 meters in length, while the maximum theoretical distance for long-haul Fibre Channel networks using fiber optic links is 10 kilometers.

Understanding Fibre Channel Topologies

The Fibre Channel standard defines three distinct *topologies*, or physical network layouts. These topologies satisfy different application and installation requirements, exhibit different performance characteristics, and are subject to different scalability limits.

▶ **Point-to-point.** The most basic Fibre Channel topology, point-to-point refers to two devices that are directly connected by a Fibre Channel cable. Addressing is simple and device availability is complete. Point-to-point Fibre Channel is not a common topology today, but it has been used to connect RAID and other storage subsystems to servers in server-centric computing environments.

▶ **Arbitrated loop.** This topology makes it possible for individual transmission paths, or loops, to be time-shared by up to 126 devices. Each time a loop is available, the devices arbitrate to determine which device gets to send data or commands next. Providing economical interconnection, Fibre Channel arbitrated loop is typically used to connect disk drives to RAID controllers or host bus adapters.

▶ **Switched fabric.** Modern SANs depend on a powerful Fibre Channel topology called *switched fabric*. A fabric essentially consists of one or more high-speed interconnection devices, or *switches*, controlling a large number of port-to-port transfers between nodes. These transfers of data and commands are called *frames*.

Fabrics function like telephone systems, which carry a number of calls simultaneously over the same wires. Within a fabric, multiple interconnections happen concurrently—and all frames are routed to their proper destinations. System-wide bandwidth can be as much as an order of magnitude greater than the speed of any single Fibre Channel link. With such high transfer rates, many users in a workflow can work with the same data at the same time without affecting performance.

Fibre Channel Addressing

Every Fibre Channel port and node has a WWN, a unique identifier that is embedded into the port or node during the manufacturing process. Vendors buy WWNs from naming authorities such as the IEEE and allocate them to devices during the manufacturing process, when they are fixed in the port hardware.

WWNNs and WWPNs

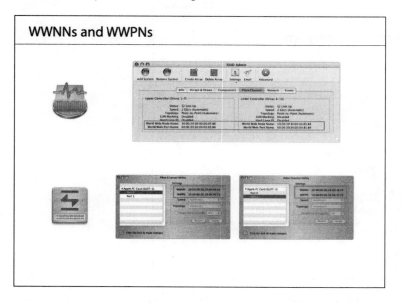

World Wide Names are distributed to vendors in blocks, similar to Ethernet MAC addresses. They are assigned to the node during the manufacturing process. Because World Wide Names are fixed in the device, they are used in Fibre Channel protocol initiation sequences. The unique identifier provided by the WWN is necessary for applications such as zoning and security.

World Wide Port Names (WWPNs) are unique for each port, and are used when connecting to a switch. World Wide Node Names (WWNNs) uniquely identify a device, and are used mainly for dual pathing software.

Along with the WWN, a Fibre Channel Port ID (FCID) is assigned to each port. Addresses are not fixed with the node but may be determined by configuration or by the protocol during initialization. FCIDs are dynamically assigned by a switch (or switch fabric), during loop initialization in FC-AL, or by the port with the lowest WWN in a point-to-point. WWNs follow a port and are used to define different information by different vendors. The specific information that must be included in each field is not defined by the Fibre Channel standard.

Fibre Channel Addressing

	Domain	Area	Port
Point-to-Point			
1 bit	0	0	1
Arbitrated Loop			
8 bits = 127 addresses per loop	0	0	AL_PA
Fibre Channel Port ID (FCID)			
24 bits = 15,663,104 addresses per fabric	10011101	1001011	10010111
Bit	23 16	15 08	07 00

Arbitrated loop devices use 8-bit addresses that are selected because of their encoded characteristics. Only 127 of the possible 256 addresses are used. AL_PA addresses may be assigned by the user for some equipment, or may be assigned by the loop during initialization.

Switched fabric uses 24-bit addressing and provides for 16,777,216 potential addresses per fabric. Several blocks of addresses are reserved for Fibre Channel functions, so the number of addresses available to connected ports is reduced to 15,663,104 (239 × 256 × 256). Addresses are assigned when a device (host or storage) logs in to the switch.

In a point-to-point connection, the port address is assigned by the port with the higher WWN, and only the port segment is used. One device takes the address 00000000, and the other device is assigned 00000001.

In a loop, each device is assigned or can be configured with an 8-bit arbitrated loop physical address (AL_PA). All NL_Ports can only communicate with each other based on the ALPA assigned to each port during the loop initialization, and the Domain and Area segments are not used. The Domain and Area fields are identical to those of the FL_Port to which the loop is connected.

Arbitrated loop devices can also be classified as *public* or *private*, depending on whether they can log in to a fabric switch. Multiple arbitrated loop hubs can be connected via *trunking*. Both of these concepts are beyond the scope of this guide.

Switched Fabric Topology

As we've said, a switched fabric topology incorporates a high-bandwidth Fibre Channel switch—instead of a hub—to handle data traffic among host and storage devices. A fabric switch uses the FC-SW (Fibre Channel-Switched fabric) protocol to communicate in this topology.

The FC-SW device addressing scheme currently allows for 15.6 million available addresses, although the practical limit is in the hundreds of thousands. The FC-SW protocol offers enhanced capabilities, including:

▶ Zoning (like virtual LANs)

▶ Security

▶ Multicast and broadcast (defined in the standard but rarely implemented)

To the nodes, the switched fabric environment appears as a single entity, no matter how many elements are actually present in the fabric. The architecture and operations of the fabric, including topology and routing, are transparent to the ports attached to the fabric.

The HBAs and array controllers do not participate in fabric operations. They talk to their connected switch port, which then takes care of fabric operations such as assigning addresses. This differs from the FC-AL architecture, where ports are responsible for loop arbitration and routing.

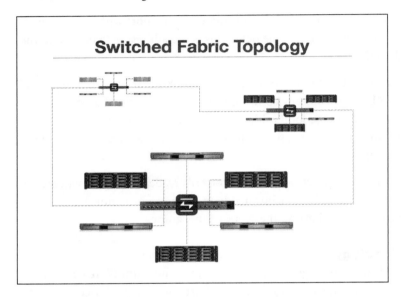

Switched Fabric Topology

There are three subsets of the switched fabric topology:

- ▶ **Cascade.** The cascade topology connects two or more fabric switches. Multiple cables between switches increase bandwidth between switches and provide redundancy should one of the interconnecting cables or ports fail.

- ▶ **Cascade loop.** A cascade loop connects three or more switches. Switches are connected in a cascade topology, but the last switch in the cascade connects to the first, to create a loop. The cascade loop allows data to transfer to its destination using the shortest path.

- ▶ **Mesh fabric.** A fully meshed fabric connects each switch to every other switch in the fabric, providing the most efficient route and the greatest redundancy.

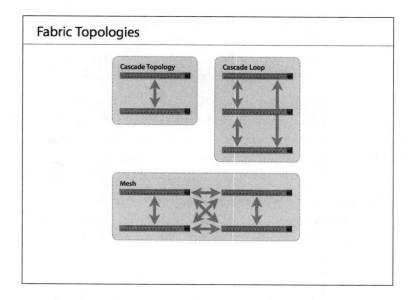

Fabric Topologies

Fibre Channel Hubs and Switches

Hubs are essentially passive wiring concentrators that provide a central point of connection for multiple devices. Hubs provide shared bandwidth: Only one pair of devices at a time can communicate with each other.

Fibre Channel hubs are roughly analogous to Ethernet hubs, in that they do not provide a switching function. They function similarly to Token Ring hubs, because the ports on the hub are connected in a physical loop (called an *arbitrated loop*).

Fibre Channel switches contain a switching matrix that can establish multiple concurrent routing paths to allow simultaneous communication between multiple sets of devices. Adding devices to a switch effectively adds bandwidth to the SAN.

Fibre Channel switches use the FC-SW protocol. All ports connected to a switch can operate at full speed. Switches have enough aggregate bandwidth to handle full-speed, full-duplex operation on every connected port.

Switches are more expensive than hubs, but they provide significantly better performance and enable a highly scalable SAN infrastructure. In addition, a switched fabric topology allows for more sophisticated network management.

Each switch in a SAN must be configured with a domain switch number and an IP address. To configure a switch, you have to know the switch's default or assigned IP address— so don't lose it. It is usually found in the user's guide for the switch. For the latest additions to this list of qualified switches, see www.apple.com/xsan/compatibility.html.

Fibre Channel switches use a nonblocking architecture that gives the switch the internal bandwidth to route frames concurrently across multiple data paths, allowing multiple devices to communicate simultaneously. Put simply, Fibre Channel networks do not slow down under heavy usage. All of the nodes connected to a switch can transmit and receive at full speed (200 MB/s over 2 Gb Fibre Channel and 400 MB/s over 4 Gb Fibre Channel).

This flexible bandwidth usage is referred to as *scalable bandwidth*. For example, if two targets and two initiators are connected to a 4 Gb switch, you could have two concurrent transactions at 400 MB/s (half-duplex), for a total of 800 MB/s throughput. If 16 devices are connected to the same 4 Gb switch, the aggregate bandwidth is 6400 MB/s.

Unlike Ethernet switches, Fibre Channel switches do not store and forward frames, which allows them to support very low latencies (typically, 0.6 µS to 3 µS). Therefore, the aggregate bandwidth increases as nodes are added.

Fabric topologies do not have the limited scalability that arbitrated loop topologies have. You'll have trouble managing the number of SAN fabric devices long before you approach device limits of the FC-SW protocol.

Understanding Xsan

Now that you have a basic understanding of storage area networks, cluster file systems, and Fibre Channel, let's move on to explore Xsan's specific implementation of these technologies. We'll examine Xsan's file system, how Xsan handles volumes and metadata, and how Xsan uses both Fibre Channel and Ethernet. We'll finish the chapter by taking a look at the unique new features of Xsan 2.

Xsan is a 64-bit cluster file system specifically designed for small and large computing environments that demand the highest level of data availability. This specialized technology enables multiple Mac desktop and Xserve systems to share RAID storage volumes over a high-speed Fibre Channel network. Each client can read and write directly to the centralized file system, accelerating user productivity while improving workgroup collaboration. Here's how the Xsan solution works.

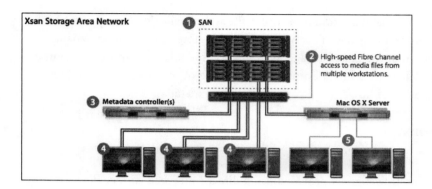

- **SAN volume.** Xsan allows you to consolidate data into a single storage volume that's accessible to all systems on the SAN. Adding capacity is as easy as attaching more RAID storage systems to your Fibre Channel network.

- **Fibre Channel network.** The SAN volume connects to the Xsan metadata controller and all Xsan clients through a high-speed Fibre Channel switch.

- **Xsan metadata controller.** Xsan includes software called the *metadata controller,* which acts as the traffic cop for the SAN. When an Xsan client attempts to read or write to a file, it gets permission from the metadata controller and then accesses the data directly on the SAN over high-speed Fibre Channel. Any Mac Pro or Xserve system running Xsan and connected to the Ethernet and Fibre Channel infrastructure can be designated the metadata controller.

- **Xsan clients.** Mac Pro or Xserve systems running Xsan have direct block-level access to files stored on the SAN volume and full read/write capability. As performance needs grow, Xsan allows you to add servers and computers to the SAN.

- **Network clients.** An Xserve with Mac OS X Server and Xsan can share data from the SAN volume with an unlimited number of networked computers over the Ethernet network using file-sharing protocols, such as AFP, SMB/CIFS, and NFS.

How the Xsan Cluster File System Works

A cluster file system is not the same thing as a SAN; it leverages the capabilities of a SAN to provide benefits such as scalability, data sharing, and storage resource management. In order to better understand cluster file systems, let's look at a few other types of file system architectures.

Understanding Xsan's implementation of a cluster file system will also force you to think about something you probably haven't considered much before: file system metadata. Xsan's implementation of metadata storage separates volume metadata from the volume data that constitutes files. To get the best use out of your resources, you need to understand what metadata is and how it is used, so we'll discuss metadata next.

Disk File Systems

Disk file systems are limited to one type of mechanism and computer:

▶ **Local file systems** are generally provided using directly attached storage devices.

▶ **Network file systems** provide some common organization, naming, and formatting, and enable sharing over some type of network.

▶ **Distributed file systems** allow arrays and groupings of remote storage to be accessed.

▶ **Cluster file systems** provide resource sharing and parallel operation.

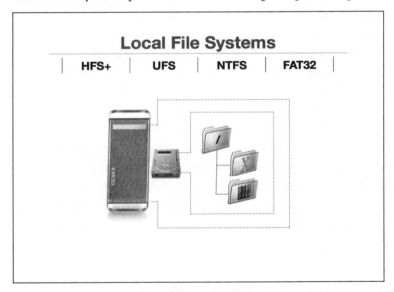

Local File Systems

A local file system views the storage as "owned" by a single computer. The local operating system finds the attached local storage assets and provides management, access, and visibility to the connected user. Usually, a tree structure is used to organize the files in a way that makes sense to the user. The local file system also defines naming conventions and data element sizes. Here are some common local file systems:

▶ **HFS+** is a hierarchical file system designed to support richer data than FAT or early UNIX.

▶ **UNIX File System (UFS)** was the original professional workstation file system from the 1970s. Today it is a stable, familiar operating system on many platforms.

▶ **Windows NT (NTFS)** was Microsoft's first entry into professional-level systems with a treed extensible file system—early 1990s vintage. It has a large installed base, is familiar to a large support base, and supports dynamic reconfiguration and fault recovery. Windows XP adopted this as the Windows XP file system in 2000, replacing the FAT (file allocation table) file system.

Network File Systems

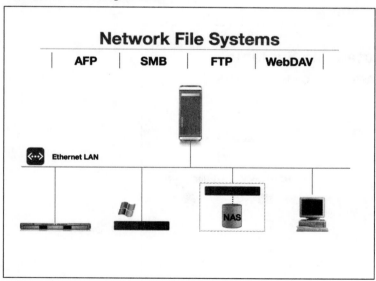

A network file system provides a methodology for files to be shared over a network connection. A single host is the owner and manager of the files. Only one user at a time can write to the file. File-element access—block-level—is not allowed.

The file system is managed by a single host. Because a single server is responsible for providing access to the file system over a network, you have a potential single point of failure. If the NAS box goes down, then all clients have lost access to the file system.

The server is the traffic bottleneck—all traffic goes through the server, with no direct access. It also is difficult and expensive to extend the storage assets beyond the amount that can be controlled by the server itself.

NFS and CIFS are file systems designed for network file sharing and are network transparent. The architecture is client/server. The storage can be consolidated, but only in one physical space.

The disadvantages of the NFS and CIFS approach are that file locking is applied one user at a time, and multiple users can't access the same data concurrently. Shared memory poses data concurrency and corruption issues. The operating system support is limited, and scaling for changing business requirements is cumbersome.

Distributed File Systems

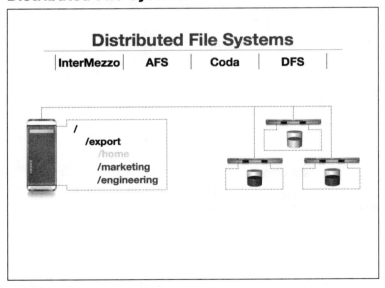

Distributed file systems are more extensible than network file systems, and they allow focused operational clustering and multiple storage assets. You can also deploy management and robustness tools like RAID, and create useful islands of storage and multiple connections to the storage. However, one computer or server is still the master. The system is designed from an access, rather than a performance, perspective. The information assets are still transferred as files, usually via the IP protocol.

Distributed file systems allow for more flexibility than disk file systems, which are implemented with the direct-attach storage architecture (DAS), but storage is still attached to a particular server. The methodology supports storage islands. Multiple servers may host the file system.

Cluster File Systems

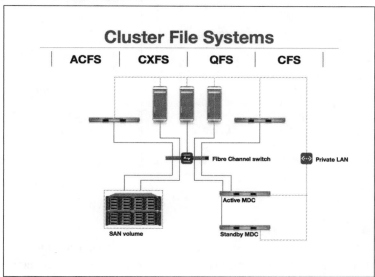

With a cluster file system, the storage assets are treated as an entity—in a cluster. The storage and file system are distributed, and not owned by a single server. Xsan is Apple's cluster file system designed for operation with Mac OS X.

This cluster approach allows multiple paths to the files and enables traffic to be balanced across servers or NAS heads. Robustness and fault tolerance are increased by the multiple pathing. The cluster file system also allows storage centralization.

The file systems are often operating system dependent. Storage and data are independent of any single server. The storage is separate and networked in a uniform file system. The file system must implement the locking mechanisms. If the file system caches data, there must be mechanisms to ensure cache coherency.

The ADIC StorNext File System is perhaps closest to Xsan. (Notably, Microsoft does not currently support this file-system methodology.)

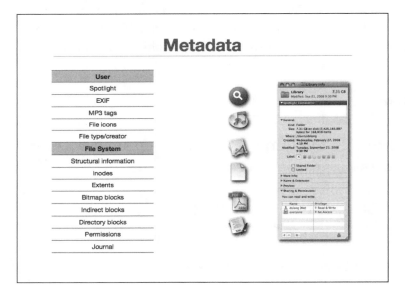

Understanding Metadata

The textbook definition of *metadata* is "data about data." If you have a background in the Mac OS, you probably associate metadata with file type and creator codes—metadata that's used by the Mac OS Finder to get information about a file and which application created it. Or you might think of the metadata contained within a file, such as the ID3 tags that are embedded in an MP3 file. These examples are not what we mean by *metadata* in the context of an Xsan.

When dealing with file systems, metadata describes how the data in a volume is organized.

Various metadata entries are used to maintain a database of where and how data is recorded on storage devices. For example, *file extent* metadata specifies which exact blocks are used to store a file. *Journal* metadata contains information about which changes are pending a file write. And *permissions* metadata define who can read and write to individual files.

Metadata and File Systems

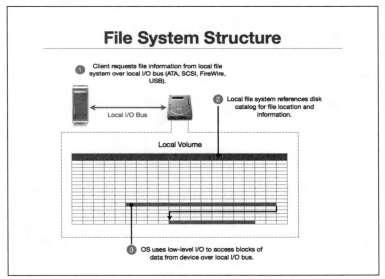

A file on a disk drive is fundamentally a stream of bytes; it can take up a single block or millions of blocks. (A storage device's *block* size defines the smallest possible chunk of data on the file system.) The blocks may or may not be contiguous.

To make sense of this stream of bytes, the file system needs to know where a file begins and ends. File extent metadata identifies the block address of the file's first block and the total number of blocks used. If the file is fragmented across noncontiguous blocks, the file system requires multiple extents to locate all the blocks used by the file.

When you are using a local file system on a DAS device, the metadata is closely tied to the file system used on the storage device, and is usually handled transparently by the file system.

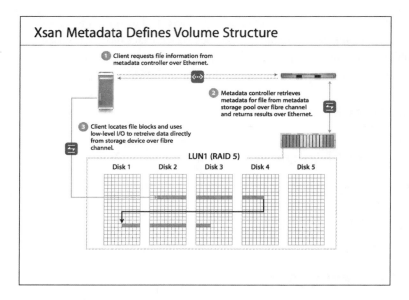

Every file system uses metadata in some form, though we don't always realize it because it's just part of the volume format. When you initialize a volume, a certain amount of space is set aside for the extents and other metadata, and there's no way to directly manipulate it. You use volume metadata every time you run the command-line tool *fsck*, which walks through each file's metadata and ensures that the metadata is consistent with the actual byte stream on the storage device.

Xsan Metadata Storage and Controllers

Designing an Xsan solution involves several important metadata-related considerations. You must choose where to store the metadata and how much space to devote to it.

You must also decide how to configure the *metadata controller*—which is the computer, typically an Xserve system, that reads, writes, and manages the metadata. Xsan requires at least one metadata controller and provides for seamless failover between additional metadata controllers to prevent service interruption and data loss.

Note that the metadata does not exist in files, because those files themselves would need metadata to define their location and size. Metadata is written in a volume-specific format. By default, it is stored on the first storage pool in the volume.

Also, most metadata does not need to be backed up separately from data, because it is specific to the storage device. When you back up a file, the backup device has its own file system with its own metadata to define how the file is stored.

Using a Metadata Ethernet Network

In a typical Xsan installation, there are two separate Ethernet networks. The public (Internet) network is used to access the Internet and file services. The private (metadata) network is specific to the SAN and is used to manage and keep track of metadata.

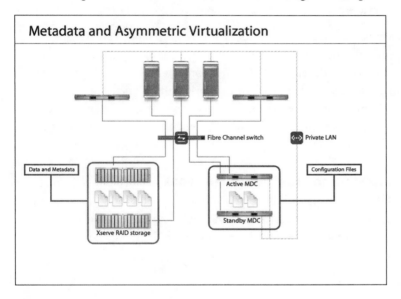

Asymmetric Virtualization

Xsan uses *asymmetric virtualization* (also known as *out-of-band* architecture) to store file metadata. Data about files—such as file names, permissions, and creation and modification dates—is stored on the SAN, but the data is accessed over the Ethernet via the metadata controller (MDC).

A private LAN network connects the metadata controller to the SAN clients and allows metadata information to be communicated between them. The Xsan Admin application also uses this Ethernet network to manage the SAN.

Meanwhile, the actual data, or file contents, is transferred across the Fibre Channel network. To prevent metadata traffic from interfering with data on the Fibre Channel network, Xsan controllers and clients exchange file system metadata over the separate Ethernet network. (Controllers do use Fibre Channel to read and write metadata on a volume.)

Why Two Separate Ethernet Networks?

Non-SAN-related Ethernet traffic can interfere with the exchange of metadata among Xsan controllers and clients. For example, using the same connection for Xsan metadata exchange and Internet access can slow file system performance. Similarly, using the same Ethernet network to access directory services and SAN metadata can reduce SAN performance.

If SAN performance is critical for your users or applications, keep all extraneous traffic off the network that clients and metadata controllers use to exchange metadata. For best SAN performance, set up a private Ethernet TCP/IP network for the exclusive use of Xsan clients and metadata controllers. For other types of network traffic—including Internet access, RAID system and Fibre Channel switch management, remote SAN management, or directory services—connect each client and metadata controller to a second Ethernet network using a second Ethernet port.

Equipment Specifications for Metadata Network

You'll examine specifications later on, but it bears repeating: All metadata controllers and clients should have the network interface attached to the metadata network configured to communicate at 1000BaseT or 1 Gb. The Ethernet switch(es) on the metadata network should provide a 1 Gb connection on each switch port and be set to Full Duplex with flow control.

Understanding the Xsan 2 Volume Structure

Now that we have a firm understanding of the underlying technology upon which Xsan is built, let's move on to Xsan itself and the structure of the Xsan 2 volume. In this section, we'll focus only on the volume and the different components of that volume. We will discuss Xsan as a file system in the next two sections.

How Xsan Storage Is Organized

Although an Xsan volume mounted on a client computer looks like a single disk, it actually consists of multiple physical disks combined on several levels using RAID techniques.

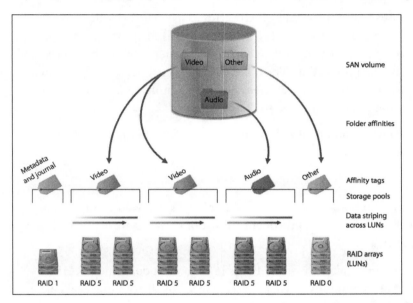

The illustration above shows how disk space provided by the individual drive modules in several RAID systems is combined into a volume that users see as a large local disk—a process called *array-based virtualization*. Here's how it works:

LUNs

The smallest storage element you work with in Xsan is a logical storage device called a *LUN* (a SCSI logical unit number). A LUN typically represents a group of drives combined into a RAID array.

You create a LUN whenever you create a RAID array on a RAID storage device. The RAID system combines individual drive modules into an array based on the RAID scheme you choose. Each array appears on the Fibre Channel network as a LUN.

Most RAID systems ship already configured as RAID arrays. The corresponding LUNs are ready to use with Xsan.

If the standard RAID arrays on your RAID systems are not right for your application, you can use the RAID system management software to re-create arrays based on other RAID schemes or different numbers of drive modules.

For example, the previous figure shows eight RAID array LUNs. The LUN that stores metadata and journal information uses RAID level 1 (mirrored) to ensure against meta-data loss. One LUN stores users' data on a RAID 0 array (striping only) for best speed and storage efficiency but no data protection. The other data LUNs use RAID 5 (distributed parity) for high performance and storage efficiency with data protection. Xsan sees the RAID arrays as LUNs that can be combined to create a volume.

Your RAID LUNs are labeled and initialized for use with the Xsan file system when you use Xsan Admin to set up a volume.

Storage Pools

LUNs are combined to form *storage pools*. A storage pool in a small volume might consist of a single RAID array, but a larger volume might consist of several storage pools, each of which includes several arrays.

Xsan distributes file data in parallel across the LUNs in a storage pool using a RAID 0 (striping) scheme. So, you can improve a client's access speed by distributing available storage over several LUNs in a storage pool.

You can set up storage pools that have different performance or recoverability character-istics based on the RAID level of their LUNs, and assign folders to them using affinities. Users can then select where to store files based on their need for speed or safety.

In the illustration, seven LUNs are combined into four storage pools for users' data. One pool uses a single RAID 0 array (fast, but not recoverable). Three other pools use multiple RAID 5 arrays (not as fast, but recoverable), and Xsan stripes data across the LUNs in each of these storage pools.

You use Xsan Admin to add available LUNs to storage pools.

Affinities

Each storage pool is assigned an affinity tag according to the pool's performance and recoverability characteristics. You can associate a folder with an affinity tag to guarantee that Xsan stores the contents of the folder on a storage pool with the desired characteristics.

More than one storage pool may have the same affinity tag. Xsan distributes the contents of a folder with a particular affinity tag among the storage pools that have that same affinity tag. This strategy improves performance when multiple users simultaneously read and write files in the same folder, because the read and write operations are distributed among the storage pools and their component LUNs.

You use Xsan Admin to assign affinity tags to storage pools and associate folders with those affinity tags.

Volumes

Storage pools are combined to create the volumes that users see. From the user's perspective, the SAN volume looks and behaves just like a large local disk, except that:

▶ The size of the volume can grow as you add underlying arrays or new storage pools.

▶ Multiple users on the SAN can access files on the volume at the same time.

In our example illustration, five storage pools are combined to create a single shared volume.

You use Xsan Admin to create volumes and mount them on client computers. The Xsan Assistant wizard guides you through the steps of creating the volume:

▶ Create the volume.

▶ Label the LUNs.

▶ Create the volume affinities.

▶ Add LUNs to storage pools.

The figure below shows how LUNs, storage pools, and volumes look as you organize them in Xsan Admin. This example shows a SAN with a single shared volume named *SanVol*. Storage for the volume is provided by three storage pools, *Meta*, *Data1*, and *Data2*—the first based on a single LUN and the others on two LUNs each.

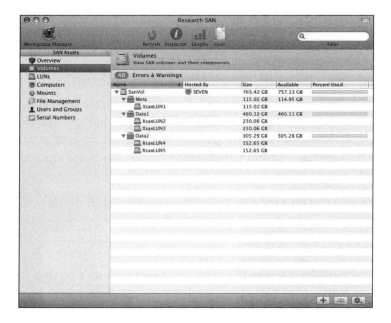

Folders with Affinities

To control which storage pools are used to store specific files (for example, to provide different levels of service for different users or applications), you can associate a folder on an Xsan volume with an affinity that is assigned to one or more of the storage pools that make up the volume.

For example, you can associate some folders with an affinity whose storage pools have faster LUNs, and associate other folders with an affinity whose storage pools have safer LUNs. Then users can choose between faster and safer storage by putting files in the appropriate folder.

In our example illustration, the Other folder has an affinity for the faster storage pool that is based on a RAID 0 array. Any file that a user copies into the Other folder is automatically stored on the faster array. The Video and Audio folders are associated with the more secure RAID 5 storage.

What's New in Xsan 2

In February 2008, Apple released Xsan 2, which added the SAN Setup Assistant, Xsan Admin 2, and MultiSAN. Xsan 2 also features enhanced monitoring tools, Spotlight integration, and support for Mac OS X Server services. Let's take a look at these new features.

Intuitive Setup and Management

Xsan 2 takes the complexity out of setting up and maintaining a SAN, while providing powerful remote management capabilities for IT and network experts. An intelligent new SAN Setup Assistant expedites the setup process for nontechnical users, with custom tools just a click away. There's also a newly designed Xsan Admin application, featuring a straightforward interface for SAN management and monitoring.

Simplified Setup

Xsan 2 handles the entire "after cable up" setup and configuration of your SAN. The SAN Setup Assistant walks you through the process—creating private metadata networks, optimizing volumes for different data types, and more. Thus, small organizations and workgroups can take advantage of a SAN and clustered network services without any networking expertise.

The simplicity starts with the out-of-the-box server setup experience. Upon installation, Mac OS X Server automatically recognizes that your system has a Fibre Channel card installed. Server Assistant asks if you want your server to be the metadata controller of a storage area network and guides you through the Xsan installation and setup process.

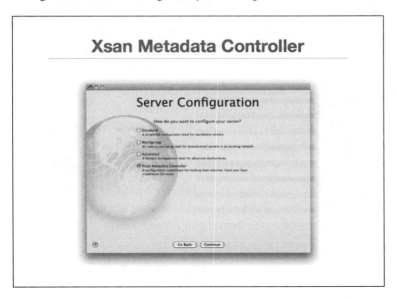

To make it easier for you to get the most performance out of your SAN, the new SAN Setup Assistant offers a choice of predefined volume configurations for common SAN scenarios. With a single click, you can organize your storage into pools optimized for the data type, file size, and file use that are typical of the scenario you select.

The options are:

▶ **HD Video:** Optimized for 720p, 1080p, and 1080i ProRes 422 or uncompressed HD video.

▶ **SD Video:** Optimized for DV, DVCAM, DVCPRO, and uncompressed SD video.

▶ **2K and 4K Video:** Optimized for 2K and 4K video.

▶ **General File Server:** Optimized for NFS, AFP, and SMB file servers.

▶ **Home Folder Server:** Optimized for NFS, AFP, and SMB home folder servers.

▶ **Mail Cluster:** Optimized for shared storage of email server data.

▶ **Podcast Producer Cluster:** Optimized for Podcast Producer video and audio data.

▶ **iCal Server Cluster:** Optimized for shared storage of calendar server data.

▶ **Final Cut Server:** Optimized for shared storage of Final Cut Server data.

▶ **Custom:** Advanced customization for expert users.

Integration with Mac OS X and Mac OS X Server

Xsan 2 leverages the power of Spotlight, making it easy and instantaneous for users to find files on massive SAN volumes—even across petabytes of data—right from the Finder. Spotlight works the way people think: by searching the content itself, not just the filenames. With richer Spotlight vocabulary in Leopard, searches can be more exact. New options include Boolean logic, quoted phrase searching, category labels, and range support. And with the Quick Look feature in Leopard, you can use Cover Flow to scan hundreds of files in just seconds, without ever needing to open them.

Key services in Mac OS X Server—iCal Server, Mail Server, and Podcast Producer—have been designed to use Xsan 2 as a clustered file system. Clustering improves network performance and scalability, while reducing the potential impact of a service outage, should any one server on the network fail.

Intuitive Remote Administration Tools

Xsan includes Xsan Admin, a complete application for remote management and monitoring of your SAN. A graphical user interface lets users on any Mac OS X or Mac OS X Server system perform administration tasks—such as creating storage pools, managing SAN volumes, setting up affinities, and assigning quotas—that would otherwise be accessible only from a command-line interface. By guiding you through these complex tasks, Xsan Admin not only facilitates SAN administration, but also reduces the chance of configuration errors.

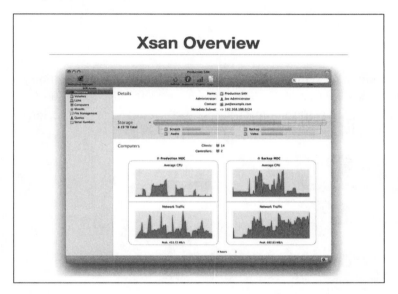

With Xsan 2 comes Xsan Admin 2, with a redesigned interface that will look and feel familiar to Mac users. The SAN assets column clearly displays volumes, LUNs, computers, and mounts. Just click to manage each component of your SAN. Context-sensitive menus change, depending on the configuration of your SAN. To identify the LUNs that you are managing, you can even use Xsan Admin to turn on the drive's activity lights. When it's time to grow your SAN, Xsan Admin 2 makes it easy to add a volume. Similarly to the original setup process, Xsan Admin asks what you're using the volume for and what you want to call it—and configures the volume accordingly.

Xsan Admin 2 prominently displays an overview of your SAN's health. With real-time monitoring, you'll always have the following information:

▶   Free space in a volume or storage pool

▶   User quota utilization

▶   Graphs of processor and network utilization

▶   Status of file system processes

▶   Log file

▶   Connected clients

▶   Fibre Channel failures

You can also use Xsan Admin to set status thresholds that trigger automatic notification via email or pager. Whether a Fibre Channel connection fails, available disk space falls below a specified level, or a critical workstation is nearing its disk quota, the notification feature enables you to respond quickly to serious problems.

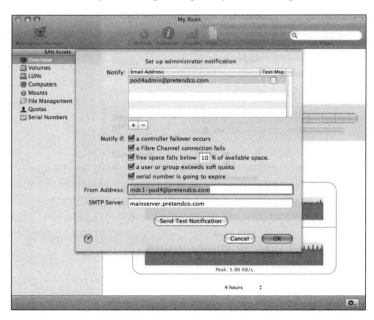

File System Capabilities

Xsan features enterprise-class SAN capabilities that meet your organization's requirements for data consolidation and fast, shared access to storage volumes.

The Xsan Cluster File System

As we've discussed, Xsan is a 64-bit cluster file system that provides concurrent data access over high-speed Fibre Channel to multiple systems on the network. For better performance and higher availability, you can pool storage across multiple RAID devices, and each Xsan client can use this centralized data as if it were directly connected. Cluster file systems of this class include SGI InfiniteStorage Filesystem CXFS and Veritas Storage Foundation Cluster File System. Here are some of the features of the Xsan cluster file system:

▶ **Support for 2 petabyte files and volumes.** Xsan lets your users share multiple files and volumes; each can be as large as 2 PB, or more than three months' worth of uncompressed 1080i high-definition (HD) video at 30 frames per second. Xsan supports billions of files per volume, with each metadata controller hosting multiple volumes at the same time.

▶ **File sharing over Fibre Channel.** Xsan storage networking eliminates the bottlenecks of traditional network file servers that use Gigabit Ethernet and are not fast enough to transfer dense formats such as HD video. Fibre Channel gives you a 4 Gb-per-port connection for increased data transfer and can be used with Fibre Channel multipathing for greater aggregate throughput. This is perfect for multiple editors working on a video project or a computer cluster that needs fast data access for maximum utilization of processing power.

▶ **File-level locking.** Fine-grained file-level locking enables simultaneous access to shared files. All clients can access all the files on the volume, but only the client that has read/write privileges can edit a locked file. This contrasts with volume-level locking, which enables only one computer at a time to write to an entire volume. File-level locking provides enormous productivity advantages in post-production workflows where multiple editors are using a single large file.

▶ **File system access controls.** Xsan supports flexible file permissions that not only work with Mac clients, but are fully compatible with Windows Server, Windows Vista, and Windows XP. With file system ACLs, any file object can be assigned multiple users and groups, including groups within groups. Each file object can also be assigned both allow and deny permissions, as well as a granular set of permissions for administrative control, read, write, and delete operations. For added security, Xsan supports a file permission inheritance model, ensuring that user permissions are inherited when files are moved to the SAN and rewritten when files are copied to the SAN.

High-Availability Features

Xsan is designed for high availability, with features that make it suitable for mission-critical environments. Metadata controller failover and Fibre Channel multipathing eliminate single points of failure, and bandwidth reservation allows you to keep bandwidth available for critical applications.

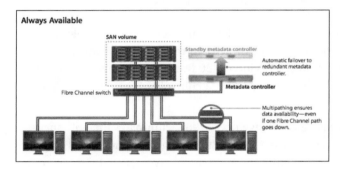

Metadata Controller Failover

If the metadata controller on your SAN fails for any reason, another computer running Xsan can take over. Metadata controller failover is built into Xsan, unlike many SAN solutions that require you to pay extra for this high-availability feature.

Xsan software includes both the metadata controller and file system client components. Using Xsan Admin 2, you can specify the "laws of succession," or the order in which Xsan metadata controllers take over for a failed controller. You can also choose a different primary metadata controller for each volume, and set up volume failover priorities to minimize the possibility of more than one volume failing over to the same metadata controller—particularly useful in MultiSAN scenarios.

Sophisticated algorithms ensure that succession occurs properly, avoiding "split brain," or multiple conflicting metadata controllers. Once the file system clients "elect" a new metadata controller, the failed system can be deactivated until the problem is resolved.

For high-volume, mission-critical production environments, you may want to dedicate a computer as a standby controller. A standby controller also enables you to update Xsan software without interrupting service to your users.

Fibre Channel Multipathing

Apple's Fibre Channel host bus adapters (HBAs) are dual-port or quad-port cards, providing every Mac Pro or Xserve system with two or four connections to the SAN. Fibre Channel multipathing takes advantage of multiple connections: If one Fibre Channel path fails, Xsan continues to use another for storage access—eliminating a potential single point of failure at the cabling layer.

All data paths from the client to the various storage volumes are discovered automatically based on load and availability. This provides two major benefits: Any failure is handled without affecting the user's work, and all paths are load-balanced to ensure maximum performance and reliability.

File System Journaling

Xsan is a journaled file system that can be recovered in seconds in the event of a server failure. Journal data includes a record of file system transactions, eliminating the need for time-consuming integrity checks after an unplanned shutdown of the entire network or of the metadata controller. Your storage can be back online immediately.

MultiSAN

In many environments, it's common to separate volumes on more than one SAN, whether to improve performance or to improve reliability and sustainability of critical data. Xsan 2 addresses this requirement with a new feature, MultiSAN. MultiSAN is a configuration in which any given MDC may host Xsan volumes that are not necessarily hosted by other MDCs. The benefit of MultiSAN is increased volume performance resulting from the distribution of volume hosting to specific metadata controllers.

For example, in video broadcast scenarios, you may have one Xsan volume for production and another for playout or broadcast. Without MultiSAN capabilities, in order to permit users to access all data, each volume would need to be hosted by the same metadata controller. If the metadata controller were to fail, both production and playout volumes would be affected. With Xsan 2 and MultiSAN, each volume can have its own metadata controller—eliminating a single point of failure—while enabling users to access both volumes. In addition, the user can continue to work on the failover system.

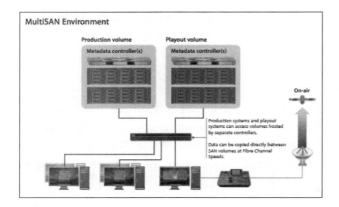

Volume Management

Flexible volume management capabilities enable you to maximize the efficiency of your storage resources. Xsan makes it easy to target data types to specific classes of storage for optimal storage performance—for example, assigning all uncompressed HD video files to one high-performance storage pool. You can then combine pools into volumes for simplified management.

For maximum performance, Xsan Admin 2 provides pre-tuned volume workload settings for different data types, file sizes, and use scenarios—ranging from very large files, such as uncompressed HD video or 2K and 4K film, to small files in data center scenarios, such as shared files or network home directories.

With the new Xsan Admin 2 application, it's easy to expand your storage resources as data needs grow: You can add LUNs and storage pools and create new volumes—without interruption in service. The downtime to grow a volume is typically just seconds.

Data Access Control

Xsan works with your directory server to help you manage file ownership and access quotas—protecting your organization's data and improving storage utilization. With LDAP integration, a central directory allows you to create consistent file system permissions across all computers accessing the storage. Other data access control features include the following:

Volume mapping

Using Xsan administration tools, you can map storage volumes to specific systems on the SAN, enabling you to define which systems can see which volumes. This protects your organization's sensitive information without getting in the way of authorized use. Although all Mac OS X file permissions still apply to Xsan, volume mapping provides an added layer of control and security.

Directory integration

Because Xsan is simply another file system, it adheres to the file system permissions built into Mac OS X, including permissions established in a central LDAP directory. Whether you use Open Directory, Active Directory, or another enterprise LDAP service, Xsan accesses information in the directory accounts that you have in place—making it easy to share permissions across computers.

If a directory service is not in place when Xsan is installed, Mac OS X Server automatically configures an Open Directory server with the metadata controller as its master—ensuring that file permissions can be properly set and managed across all systems. With file system ACLs, any file object can be assigned multiple users and groups, including groups within groups.

Control over access permissions

You can use Xsan Admin to set user and group permissions, as well as access privileges, at several levels:

▶ Restrict user access to folders on a volume by specifying owner, group, and general access permissions.

▶ Unmount a SAN volume from selected client computers.

▶ Restrict a client computer to read-only access to a volume.

▶ Remove a client from a SAN.

Disk quotas

LDAP integration also makes it easy to manage disk space quotas. You can assign quotas to users, groups, applications, or any combination of the three. Xsan enforces two types of quotas for each user, group, or application:

▶ **Soft quota.** The soft quota is the maximum space a user or group is expected to occupy on a regular basis. Users can exceed their soft quota, for a specified grace period only, up to their hard quota.

▶ **Hard quota.** The hard quota is an absolute limit on the space a user or group can occupy. Users are prevented from using more space than specified by their hard quota.

Users or groups can exceed their soft quota provided that they drop below it at some point during the grace period you specify. If users or groups exceed their soft quota for longer than the grace period, the soft quota changes to a hard quota; they will not be able to save additional data on the volume until they delete old files and drop below the soft quota.

Quotas are set individually for each volume in a SAN. To establish clear limits, you can set the soft quota, hard quota, and grace period in combination—while still allowing temporary access to extra space for unexpected storage needs. Users for whom no quotas are specified can use all available space on a volume.

Compatibility and Interoperability

Xsan lets you create a SAN that is compatible with your existing infrastructure, giving you the flexibility to build a system that's right for your organization, while maximizing the return on your storage investment.

▶ **Support for native Mac OS X applications.** Xsan is designed to support most native Mac OS X and UNIX applications, and delivers incredible performance on Mac Pro and Xserve systems. For maximum flexibility and compatibility with non-Apple systems, it uses a case-sensitive, single-fork file system.

▶ **Fibre Channel infrastructure integration.** Apple has qualified several of the most popular Fibre Channel switches for use with an Xsan network. These include the QLogic SANbox product line, the Cisco MDS 9000 family, and the Brocade SilkWorm series.

▶ **Quantum integration.** In heterogeneous computing environments, you can add non–Mac OS X clients to your Xsan network using the StorNext File System. Computers running the StorNext File System can access Xsan volumes directly over high-speed Fibre Channel—without any modification. In addition, Mac and Xserve clients with Xsan can be added to an existing StorNext-based SAN environment.

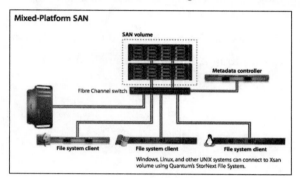

The StorNext Management Suite also supports Xsan deployments. This policy-based information lifecycle management (ILM) solution can be used in conjunction with the Scalar line of tape libraries, offering a robust tape backup option for your Xsan volumes.

What You've Learned

▶ The three main network storage architectures, how they work, and their characteristics.

▶ To identify the benefits of storage networking and the application of storage networking technologies and the SAN architecture in particular.

▶ What components are required when creating a SAN and the underlying technologies involved when deploying a SAN solution.

▶ Cluster file systems are uniquely able to take advantage of a SAN storage architecture.

▶ There are key features to a SAN, including the components required and their distinguishing characteristics.

▶ Fibre Channel and its underlying technology is uniquely suited for a SAN environment.

▶ Having a separate Ethernet for the private metadata network, though not absolutely required, is highly recommended, and the separation of network traffic between the SAN and a public network could greatly enhance the performance of the SAN in high-bandwidth environments.

▶ There are a number of SAN technologies, and Xsan is just one implementation of that technology.

▶ You are able to describe the basic structure of an Xsan volume and the Xsan file system.

▶ There are a number of new features with Xsan 2. Among these are MultiSAN and Spotlight.

References

Administration Guides

Xsan 2 Setup Guide
(http://images.apple.com/xsan/docs/Xsan_2_Setup_Guide.pdf)

Xsan 2 Administrator's Guide
(http://images.apple.com/xsan/docs/Xsan_2_Admin_Guide.pdf)

Xsan 2 Technology Overview March 2008
(http://images.apple.com/xsan/docs/L363053A_Xsan2_TO.pdf)

Xsan 1.4 Reference Guide

Apple Knowledge Base Documents

"Xsan 2 or later: How to configure MultiSAN"
(http://support.apple.com/kb/HT3144)

Review Questions

1. What are the system requirements when using Promise Storage and Xsan 2?

2. The key to a Fibre Channel fabric is the Fibre Channel switch; what factors should you consider when specifying a switch?

3. The maximum cable run from a client to an Ethernet switch should be no greater than what?

4. When purchasing fiber optic connectors, why should you make sure that they are qualified for use in a Fibre Channel network?

5. Should a controller on a Promise VTrak fail, what happens to the LUNs associated with that controller?

6. Why is a network time server recommended for Xsan deployments?

7. How does the deployment of directory services assist with user and group management?

8. Why is it not recommended to have multiple LUNs associated with more than one RAID controller?

Answers

1. When using Promise VTrak storage with Xsan 2, your system must be configured with an Intel processor and either Mac OS X v10.5.2 or Mac OS X Server v10.5.2.

2. Port density, expandability, speed, management, and power.

3. 100 meters.

4. Fiber optic connectors for both Ethernet and Fibre Channel look the same. However, they support different protocols.

5. The second controller in the RAID takes over the management of those LUNs until the first controller is replaced.

6. Having all clients bound to the same network time server helps to keep files and processes that rely on date or time stamps in sync.

7. Directory services allows for the centralization of user and group management.

8. Generally, the more LUNs associated with a controller, the lower the bandwidth available to each LUN. On an Xserve RAID, multiple LUNs on a controller could have a serious impact on the performance of that LUN and storage pool. However, with the Promise VTrak, the performance of the controller has been improved by four times the amount of bandwidth available on an Xserve RAID controller. Therefore, the number of LUNs per controller is not as critical.

2

Time   This chapter takes approximately 2 hours to complete.

Goals   Plan the layout and organization of a SAN

Identify the system requirements for Xsan 2 and the Fibre Channel components necessary for an Xsan deployment

Learn Ethernet and fiber cable distance limits

Understand Ethernet and Fibre Channel GBIC compatibilities

Identify the storage devices supported by Xsan 2

Identify the benefits of deploying Domain Name Services, directory services, and a central time server with Xsan 2

Determine the setup and performance characteristics of various Xsan 2 volume configurations

Consider the factors involved in setting up Xsan 2 volumes

Chapter 2

Planning Xsan Deployments

It's easy to add storage to an existing Xsan SAN, but reorganizing a SAN after you've set it up is not so simple. Therefore, it's important to plan the layout and organization of your SAN and its storage in advance.

An Xsan SAN is made up of the following:

▶ Storage devices (RAID systems)

▶ LUNs (SCSI logical unit numbers, usually RAID arrays)

▶ Storage groups (groups of LUNs)

▶ Affinity tags, which identify storage pools with similar performance and data protection

▶ Volumes (groups of storage pools visible to users)

▶ Clients (computers that use volumes)

▶ Controllers (computers that manage volume metadata)

▶ An Ethernet network used to exchange volume metadata

▶ A Fibre Channel network used to transfer data to and from volumes

Before you set up a SAN, you need to decide how you will configure these components. Take the time to create a diagram or a table that organizes available hardware into RAID arrays, volumes, client computers, and metadata controllers to meet SAN users' needs and your needs as the SAN administrator. For example, you won't need to plan your storage pools or affinity tags if you set up each volume using a preset volume type based on the kind of work the volume will support.

After mastering this chapter, you should be able to identify the hardware and software required to successfully deploy a bandwidth-intensive Xsan network.

Choosing Xsan Components

Your SAN environment needs to satisfy requirements in these areas:

► Supported computers

► Supported storage devices

► Ethernet network

► Fibre Channel fabric, adapters, and switches

► Directory services (optional)

► Outgoing mail service (optional)

Supported Computers

When planning for the Xsan deployment, remember that only computers in which a Fibre Channel card can be installed can be used as SAN clients. If a Fibre Channel card cannot be installed, that computer could still access the data on the SAN; however, it would have to do so through an Ethernet connection to a SAN client.

Supported Storage Devices

You can use Xsan 2 with storage devices qualified by Apple. Currently, only two devices are qualified to work with Xsan 2: Xserve RAID and the Promise VTrak E-Class/Promise-VTrak J-Class. The Xserve RAID is no longer shipping, which leaves the Promise RAIDs as the only solution qualified for new SAN deployments. For the most current information about qualified RAID systems, see the Xsan web page at www.apple.com/xsan.

Fibre Channel Fabric

File content in an Xsan SAN is transferred over Fibre Channel connections (as is the volume metadata used by controllers). The Fibre Channel fabric is the key to a SAN, as it enables sharing storage among many clients.

Ethernet TCP/IP Network

Xsan controllers and clients exchange file system metadata over an Ethernet network rather than Fibre Channel. So, computers on the SAN must also be connected to an Ethernet network.

Directory Services

If you plan to use user and group privileges to control access to files and folders on the SAN, you should set up or join a central directory of users and groups. A central directory service allows you to manage all SAN users and groups from one computer rather than individually visiting and configuring each SAN client and metadata controller.

Outgoing Mail Service

Xsan can send SAN status notifications via email on your local network (IP subnet) without using a separate mail server. However, to send notifications outside your local network, you need an SMTP server to act as a mail gateway. If you don't have access to an outgoing mail server, you can use the mail service in Mac OS X Server. For information, see *Mail Service Administration* on the Apple Servers Resources page (www.apple.com/server/resources).

Configuring Clients

When choosing workstations and servers, be aware that all Xsan clients and controllers must have Fibre Channel ports, but only the Mac Pro and Xserve have this hardware.

In addition, the higher-than-average complexity of SAN networks makes component compatibility very important. Therefore, using Apple-certified gear is highly recommended.

You can deploy Xsan 2 on computers that meet these minimum requirements:

Base Systems

▶ Mac Pro, Xserve or Power Mac with an Intel processor or PowerPC G5 processor for use with Xsan 2 and Xserve RAID

▶ Mac Pro, Xserve with an Intel processor for use with Xsan 2 and Promise RAID. The Power Mac or Xserve with a PowerPC G5 processor is not supported with Promise RAIDs.

Memory

▶ Client computers need at least 2 gigabytes of RAM (clients with Xsan 1.4.2 and Mac OS X v10.4.11 or Mac OS X Server v10.4.11 require at least 1 GB of RAM).

▶ Computers used as metadata controllers need at least 2 GB of RAM for the operating system and 2 GB of RAM for each SAN volume hosted by the controller.

Supported Operating Systems

▶ You can install Xsan 2 only on computers running Mac OS X v10.5 or Mac OS X Server v10.5.

▶ Promise VTrak storage requires Xsan 2.0 and Mac OS X v10.5.2 or Mac OS X Server v10.5.2.

▶ Mac client computers running Xsan 1.4.2 can join an Xsan 2 SAN. These clients can have 10.4.11 or 10.5.2.

▶ To join an Xsan 2 SAN, Windows, AIX, IRIX, Linux, and Solaris clients must be running Quantum's StorNext File System version 2.8 or better. For complete compatibility information, see Apple's Knowledge Base article "Xsan: Compatibility of SAN clients with Xsan and StorNext controllers" (http://support.apple.com/kb/HT1517).

Considering Network Devices and Connections

Fibre Channel and Ethernet networks are the components that connect your devices. You cannot have a SAN environment without using them. Fibre Channel is required to transfer data from client to storage and storage to client. Ethernet is required to pass along metadata information between the controllers and clients.

Setting Up a Fibre Channel Network

Unlike file system metadata, which controllers and clients exchange over Ethernet, actual file content in an Xsan SAN is transferred over Fibre Channel connections (as is metadata that controllers access on a volume). To set up the connections, you need the following:

▶ An Apple Fibre Channel PCI, PCI-X, or PCI-E card for each client and controller computer

▶ An Apple-qualified Fibre Channel switch

▶ Fibre Channel cables to connect computers and storage devices to switches forming a Fibre Channel fabric

As with any network implementation, successful deployment requires that you carefully determine needs, understand technical requirements and trade-offs, and choose the optimal configurations and components for your situation.

To begin, you can decide which type of Fibre Channel network will best suit your needs by answering a few questions. For example:

▶ Are you building a new network or expanding an existing one?

▶ What will be the network's total physical length?

▶ How many devices will be networked?

Providing detailed answers to questions like these will help determine the optimal physical layout and specifications of your network, including the type of cabling and the type and number of components and connectors you will need.

Choosing Copper or Fiber Optic Cables

Choosing the type of overall network interconnection—copper or fiber optic—is crucial. The decision usually depends upon the distances between the Fibre Channel devices. Apple Fibre Channel PCI cards, when equipped with long-haul transceivers, permit use of fiber optic cables up to 500 meters in length.

Copper cabling performs as well as fiber optic when the distance between devices is 2.9 meters or less. This cabling is typical in point-to-point and other topologies when devices are mounted in the same rack or located near each other in the same room.

Copper cables are durable, are easy to work with, and can withstand being stepped on or pulled. They're also inexpensive to purchase, install, and maintain.

Fiber optic–based Fibre Channel networks cost more and are more complicated to deploy than copper-based ones. But fiber optic cables are necessary to achieve the high data rates of Fibre Channel when servers and other network devices are located more than 2.9 meters apart—for example, in different buildings or on different floors of a building.

It's not just the cabling that contributes to the cost and complexity of fiber optic installations. Cable runs require transceivers at each end, and the brand and type must be specified correctly. Some are short haul, some are long haul (over 150 meters), and none are cheap.

Fiber optic cables are immune to the electrical resistance and electromagnetic interference (EMI) problems that affect signals carried over a copper network. However, dirt, dust, and moisture can significantly diminish signal strength in fiber optic cabling, as will material defects in the glass fiber or damage to it caused by inexpert handling and installation.

Fiber optic cables are available in two types: single-mode fiber at a diameter of 9 microns, and multimode fiber at a diameter of 50 or 62.5 microns. Your Fibre Channel integrator or installer can tell you which type is best for your network. After installation, make sure your installer tests the cabling to verify that it is not broken and will deliver maximum performance. Variation in cable performance can have a significant impact on the performance of the entire network.

Optical fiber transmission media is naturally fragile. Curl a loop of fiber optic cable and the glass core is likely to fracture microscopically. Such fractures—as well as any scratches, nicks, or imperfections in the glass itself—disperse some of the light passing through the core, thereby reducing the strength of the signal carrying the data. This loss in signal strength, called *attenuation*, has to be minimized throughout the network.

Fiber optic–cable installation requires great care, special tools, and expertise. To ensure maximum network performance, engage a certified fiber optic installer to do the work. Make sure the installer has a cable tester that will check for high levels of throughput in each section of the network.

Using Critical Connectors

To select the correct fiber optic connectors, you need to know what the cables are connecting. For example, nearly all Fibre Channel switches require SFP (*small form factor pluggable*) interconnect cables. In 2 Gbit and 4 Gbit networks, the SFPs use a connector technology designated *LC*; in older 1 Gbit networks, they use a connector technology designated *SC*.

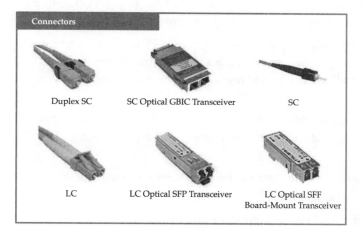

Installation methods vary, but all share certain cautions. For example, when stripping the cable's outer jacket and fiber coating, the installer must use special techniques and tools to avoid damaging the glass fiber. To ensure long-term, consistent performance and reliability, it's also important to avoid touching the end face of the fiber after the connector is attached.

Depending on the current connectors and Fibre Channel hardware in your deployment, you will probably need to order specific HBAs (Host Bus Adapters), connectors, or switches. To assist in determining which Fibre Channel hardware is compatible in your environment, you should consult the *Fibre Channel Hardware Compatibility Guide* (http://support.apple.com/kb/HT1769).

Although the fiber optic GBIC, SFP, and SFF connectors for Fibre Channel are similar in appearance to the same fiber optic connectors used with Ethernet networks, these connectors do not support the same protocols and are not compatible.

Selecting Fibre Channel Switches

Apple has certified a number of Fibre Channel switches from Brocade, Cisco, and QLogic. You can find more information on these switches at Apple's Xsan Compatibility page (www.apple.com/xsan/resources/compatibility.html). When selecting a Fibre Channel switch, you should ask the following questions:

▶ Port Density: Based on the number of nodes on your Fibre Channel network, will the switch have enough ports to satisfy your design requirements?

▶ Expandability: Is a particular switch capable of growing your Fibre Channel fabric as you add more clients? Or will you have to purchase a larger switch? Does the switch offer a stacking feature that allows you to add more of the same switches when you need to grow your fabric?

▶ Speed: Is the port speed on the switch equal to or faster than the speed of the Fibre cards installed in your clients, and will those ports auto-negotiate to slower speeds if necessary?

▶ Management: What tools are available from the manufacturer for managing the switch and customizing the configurations?

▶ Power: Does the switch offer dual power supplies in case of failure?

Your answers to these questions will help you to determine the correct switch for your deployment.

Planning the Ethernet TCP/IP Network

All Xsan computers must be able to communicate via an Ethernet network. While most file-transfer operations occur over Fibre Channel, Ethernet is used to communicate the information required to use the Xsan file system. If you also use Ethernet to access a LAN, access the Internet, or share files, it is strongly recommended that you have two Ethernet networks: one for general network access and one dedicated to Xsan.

If SAN performance is critical for your users or applications, keep all extraneous traffic off the network that clients and metadata controllers use to exchange metadata. For best SAN performance, set up a private Ethernet TCP/IP network for the exclusive use of Xsan clients and metadata controllers. For other types of network traffic—including Internet access, RAID system and Fibre Channel switch management, remote SAN management, or directory services—use a second Ethernet port to connect each client and metadata controller to a second Ethernet network.

Ethernet connections serve several functions in an Xsan storage area network:

- ▶ Xsan clients and metadata controllers use Ethernet to exchange volume metadata.
- ▶ Xsan clients can use Ethernet for access to networks outside the SAN (campus or corporate intranet or the Internet).
- ▶ Xsan metadata controllers can use Ethernet connections for remote management.
- ▶ RAID systems can use Ethernet connections for switch management.

To address all of those functions, you have your choice of two options:

- ▶ Use one Ethernet network for all traffic. This is the less expensive option, but it is also less secure and might not provide the best possible performance.
- ▶ Use two separate networks—one for metadata and another for all other IP traffic. This configuration is slightly more expensive (requiring two Ethernet adapters for each computer), but it offers greater security and better performance because routine network traffic does not interfere with SAN volume metadata traffic.

Using a Public Ethernet Network

The public Ethernet network is your public LAN. This is the network that your users will access when connecting to directory services, the Internet, file servers, and so on. It is also the network that you will use to manage the hardware associated with your SAN. In general, every component—servers, workstations, storage, Fibre Channel switches, and so on—will be connected to the public Ethernet network. Each of these devices will need to have its own IP address and should have its own specific DNS (Domain Name System) records.

When planning a public Ethernet network, you should consider the following:

- ▶ The Ethernet switches you choose for your public Ethernet network may be decided for you by policies governed by your company or institution. If that is the case, you should request that the switch be at least a 1000Base-T or 1 Gbit switch.
- ▶ Each of the devices on your SAN should have static (fixed) IP addresses for Ethernet network connections. For the public intranet and Internet connection, you can enter each computer's static IP address, subnet mask, router address, and DNS server

address manually, or configure a DHCP server to provide some or all of this information. If you want the DHCP server to provide IP addresses, it must always assign the same static IP address to the same SAN device. Don't use DHCP to assign dynamic IP addresses to SAN devices.

▶ When running the cable for your public network, it is always best to have as few "hops" as possible. Therefore, you should try to connect all cables to a primary switch. Obviously, this is not always possible because distances and facilities sometimes dictate the need to cascade multiple switches off a single master switch. If it is necessary to connect SAN devices to multiple Ethernet switches, make sure that the connection between the switches is at least as fast as the connection between the switch and the device. It is also important to limit cable runs to 100 meters. Over 100 meters, you are likely to have signal degradation.

Using a Private Metadata Ethernet Network

Client workstations use the private metadata network to communicate with the metadata controller(s) to access data about files stored on the SAN. This information includes filenames, permissions, and creation and modification dates. Remember, the metadata controllers do *not* access metadata information via the private metadata network. Metadata controllers access this information via fiber directly from the SAN. Any latency in this network could cause delays in the communication between the client and the metadata controller, and reduce the performance of your SAN. For instance, in a high-bandwidth video environment, this latency may cause dropped frames.

When planning your private Ethernet network, you should consider the following:

▶ The Ethernet switches you choose for your private Ethernet network may be decided for you by policies governed by your company or institution. If that is the case, you should request that the switch be at least a 1000Base-T or 1 Gbit switch. Also, these switches should not be connected to the public Ethernet network in any way. They should be completely isolated from all other network traffic and used solely for metadata communication.

▶ For the SAN metadata network, SAN computers should have static private (non-routable) IP addresses, unless you're unable to set up a separate, private Ethernet network for SAN metadata. If you're setting up new computers or computers on which you have just performed a clean installation of Mac OS X v10.5.2 or Mac OS X v10.5.2 Server, you can configure Xsan Admin to assign and manage addresses for your private metadata network. If you choose to assign addresses manually, use one of the following ranges of IP addresses on your private (non-routed) metadata network:

Private address range	Associated subnet mask	Comments
10.0.0.0–10.255.255.255	255.0.0.0	10/8
172.16.0.0–172.31.255.255	255.240.0.0	172.16/12
192.168.0.0–192.168.255.255	255.255.0.0	192.168/16

▶ As with the cabling for the public network, you should try to avoid "hops" if possible and keep the cable runs within 100 meters of the Ethernet switch.

Planning Storage

In Xsan 2, Apple introduced support for the first third-party RAID product. Promise Technology's VTrak E-Class and J-Class are both qualified for Xsan 2 and Final Cut Studio 2. Additionally, Apple has discontinued the Xserve RAID. However, though discontinued, the Xserve RAID still represents a large number of Xsan installations throughout the world. Therefore, the inclusion of Xserve RAIDs in Xsan 2 SANs is warranted. If you intend to use Xserve RAIDs and Promise RAIDs in the same Xsan volume, make sure that you use the same RAID type and configuration in individual storage pools. Do not mix Promise RAIDs and Xserve RAIDs in the same storage pools.

Understanding Xserve RAID

The Xserve RAID provides large storage capacities with a very low cost per megabyte by using 14 independent Ultra ATA channels to ATA drives. It has two independent hardware RAID controllers, each with a dedicated 2 Gbit Fibre Channel interface that supports 200 megabytes per second throughput per channel (400 MB/s in full duplex). Each controller manages seven drive channels on each side. It supports RAID 0, 1, 3, 5, and 0+1, and provides a Java-based RAID Admin application to set up and monitor the RAID.

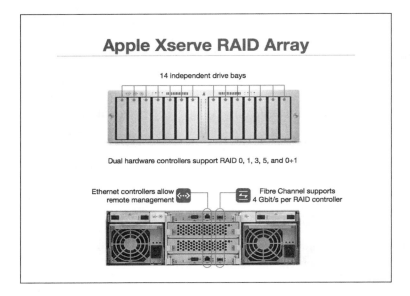

The Xserve RAID uses a dedicated ATA/100 channel for each of its 14 drive bays. This drive independence prevents data bottlenecks and maximizes throughput while enhancing data availability. Because each hard drive is isolated on its own bus, a drive failure doesn't degrade the accessibility or performance of the surviving drives. Independent drive channels also reduce the complexity and cost of high-availability storage because loop redundancy circuits and signal amplifiers aren't required, as they are in multidrive Fibre Channel and SCSI implementations.

Each Apple Drive Module is equipped with 8 MB of disk cache to accelerate read-and-write operations in performance-sensitive applications such as video editing. An on-drive read cache, commonly called a *read-ahead cache*, allows the drive controller to retrieve a block of data before it is requested by the host system. Using an on-drive write cache is inherently risky; in the event of a power failure, the cached data could be lost. For this reason, it is turned off by default in protected RAID configurations.

Xserve RAID features dual, independent hardware RAID controllers, each with a 2 Gbit Fibre Channel port for fast data transport between the storage system and the host computer. This industry-standard technology provides superior bandwidth, availability, and deployment flexibility over SCSI technology. Each 2 Gbit Fibre Channel port offers 200 MB/s bandwidth for a total throughput of up to 400 MB/s per Xserve RAID storage device.

Understanding Promise VTrak

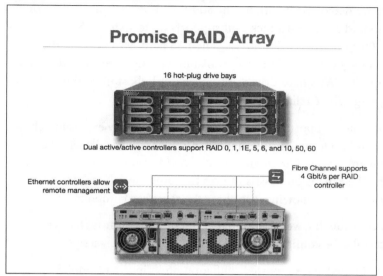

The Promise VTrak E-Class RAID was qualified for use with Xsan 2 and Final Cut Studio 2 in spring 2008 and effectively replaced the Xserve RAID as the storage of choice for Xsan. The VTrak E-Class RAID features dual active/active RAID controllers, dual 4 Gbit/s Fibre Channel ports per controller, support for SATA and SAS hard drives, and support for multiple RAID levels, and allows you to add an expansion chassis to increase storage.

The advanced subsystem design includes fully redundant, active/active hot-swappable controllers and load-balanced power and cooling units. All system components are monitored for continuous operation and send instant user notification in case of failure or malfunction. The active/active RAID controllers balance the workload across the data paths in normal operation, and provide redundant data paths and high availability in the event of a controller failure.

Each RAID features dual active/active hot-swappable RAID controllers with failover/failback, each with two 4 Gbit Fibre Channel host interface ports per controller. Each 4 Gbit Fibre Channel port offers 400 MB/s bandwidth for a total throughput of up to 1600 MB/s for each Promise RAID. It also supports RAID 0, 1, 1E, 5, 6, 10, 50, 60, and any simultaneous combination of these RAID levels. Each controller can manage the entire RAID with up to 256 RAID levels and array types in any combination.

By simultaneously supporting both SAS and SATA drives in the same chassis, the Promise VTrak allows a tiered storage deployment without the additional cost of specific SAS or SATA hardware. Each standard 3U 19-inch rack unit supports up to sixteen 15,000 rpm 3.5-inch SAS drives or 7200 rpm SATA 3 Gbit drives. The SAS hard drives deliver the speed, reliability, and scalability demanded in high-availability or high-performance environments. The higher-capacity SATA hard drives prove ideal for bulk storage applications by combining low-cost-per-gigabyte reliability and scalability.

The Promise VTrak E-Class also supports the addition of a single, 16-bay expansion chassis for video applications, and up to four additional expansion chassis for data applications. Dual I/O modules with 4x wide SAS interconnects provide redundant connectivity and 12 Gbit/s bandwidth. The expansion chassis utilizes the same mechanical design as the VTrak E-Class RAID subsystem, allowing it to share the same key components.

The RAID can be managed through a web-based management tool or through a serial connection. The RAID can also be configured by importing configuration scripts.

Apple provides a number of tested and supported configuration scripts that simplify system configuration for most common Mac OS X storage applications, including Xsan configurations. These scripts automatically configure a new VTrak system for best performance.

Visit Apple's Knowledge Base article "Promise VTrak: Configuring for optimal performance" (http://support.apple.com/kb/HT1200) for configuration scripts and directions on applying them.

More information on the Promise VTrak series of RAIDs qualified by Apple can be found at www.promise.com/apple.

Planning Network Services

In addition to storage, your network will need to provide users with services to enable Internet access, accurately track time and time stamps, and send email.

Setting Up a Domain Name Service

When your clients want to connect to a network resource such as a web or file server, they typically request it by its domain name (such as www.example.com) rather than its IP address (such as 192.168.12.12). The Domain Name System (DNS) is a distributed database that maps IP addresses to domain names so that your clients can find the resources by name rather than numerical address.

A DNS server maintains a list of domain names and the IP addresses associated with those names. When a computer needs to find the IP address for a domain name, it sends a message to the DNS server, which is also known as a *name server*.

The name server looks up the IP address and sends it back to the computer. If the name server doesn't have the IP address locally, it sends messages to other name servers on the Internet until the IP address is found.

Setting up and maintaining a DNS server is a complex process. Therefore, if you have concerns about correctly setting up DNS, Apple can help locate a network consultant to implement a DNS service. Contact Apple Professional Services and Apple Consultants Network on the web at www.apple.com/services or at http://consultants.apple.com.

If you feel comfortable configuring your own DNS server, you'll need to decide whether to configure the DNS server using Server Admin or by editing the BIND configuration file. Unless you are experienced, Server Admin is the recommended tool.

When creating DNS entries for the devices on the SAN, you must also create a DNS entry for each client's private metadata interface. In the following image, for example, the public interface of the metadata controller mdc1.pretendco.san is 172.16.10.1, while the private metadata interface of the metadata controller mdc1-private.pretendco.san is 192.168.1.1.

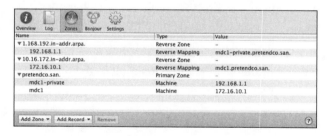

In this example, both interfaces are in the same zone (pretendco.san). However, you can also configure a separate zone for the private metadata IP addresses.

Creating a DNS entry may seem unnecessary because the private metadata network is not connected to the public network, and no router or DNS entry in the private metadata interface exists on any of the SAN clients. However, although there is no external connection via the private metadata network, the SAN client will expect the private address to be resolved by a DNS server. When the 192.168.1.1 address is not found on the DNS server, the DNS server will forward the request to a DNS server on the Internet. Forwarding will take time and can delay system functions as the client waits for the resolution to take place. This waiting can be eliminated by adding a DNS entry for the private address.

Using a Network Time Server

From shared file systems to billing services, correct timekeeping is a necessity. However, clocks on computers throughout a network can have widely different time stamps. Network Time Protocol (NTP) is used to synchronize the clocks in networked computers to a single reference clock. NTP ensures that all computers on a network report the same time.

If an isolated network (or even a single computer) is unsynchronized, services that use time and date stamps (such as mail service, or web service with timed cookies) will send wrong time and date stamps and lose synchronization with other computers across the Internet.

For example, an email message could arrive minutes (or years) before it was sent (according to the time stamp), and a reply to that message could appear to arrive before the original was sent.

Having all of your SAN clients pointing to the same Network Time Server will greatly improve logging accuracy and performance of Directory Services. The improvement is especially noticeable when using network or portable home folders. When a client is out of sync with the Open Directory master or any other directory services controller, the issue may manifest itself when the user is no longer able to log in to other workstations.

In general, having a local Network Time Server running internally on your own network will lead to machines syncing faster, syncing more reliably, and remaining in tighter sync, compared with accessing an external NTP server.

Administering Mail Services

Xsan can send SAN status notifications via email on your local network (IP subnet) without using a separate mail server. However, to send notifications outside your local network, you need a Simple Mail Transfer Protocol (SMTP) server to act as a mail gateway. If you don't have access to an outgoing mail server, you can configure the mail service in Mac OS X Server. For information, see *Mail Service Administration* on the Mac OS X Server Resources page (www.apple.com/server/macosx/resources).

Providing Directory Services

If you already have directory services provided by an Open Directory server, you can employ the setup assistant to configure each metadata controller and client computer with Xsan 2 to use existing user and group accounts from the Open Directory server. If you have another type of directory service, such as Active Directory, you can configure each controller and client to connect to it for user and group accounts by using the Directory Utility application after initial setup. If you have client computers with Mac OS X v10.4.11, you can use the Directory Access application on each one to connect it to a directory server.

If your SAN doesn't have access to an existing directory service, during the initial setup of your Xsan primary metadata controller, you can specify that you want to use Xsan Admin to manage your users and groups. The setup assistant creates an Open Directory master server on your primary metadata controller and sets up Open Directory replica servers on your standby metadata controllers. The Open Directory master provides an LDAP directory, single sign-on user authentication using Kerberos, and password validation using common authentication methods. The replicas improve responsiveness and provide automatic failover of Open Directory services.

The setup assistant also configures Xsan 2 client computers to connect to your Xsan primary metadata controller for Open Directory user and group accounts. If you have client computers with Mac OS X v10.4.11, you will need to use the Directory Access application on each client to connect it to your Xsan primary metadata controller's Open Directory service.

If you need to set up an Open Directory server manually, use Mac OS X Server's Server Admin application. Then, use the Workgroup Manager application to manage users and groups. For information, see the *Open Directory Administration* and *User Management* guides on the Mac OS X Server Resources page (www.apple.com/server/macosx/resources).

Using Server Admin, you can configure Mac OS X Server as an Open Directory master so that it can provide directory information and authentication information to other systems.

Mac OS X Server provides directory information by hosting a shared LDAP directory domain. In addition, the server authenticates users whose accounts are stored in the shared LDAP directory domain.

An Open Directory master has an Open Directory password server, which supports all conventional authentication methods required by Mac OS X Server services. In addition, an Open Directory master can provide Kerberos authentication for single sign-on.

If you want the Open Directory master to provide Kerberos authentication for single sign-on, DNS must be available on the network and correctly configured to resolve the fully qualified DNS name of the Open Directory master server to its IP address. DNS must also be configured to resolve the IP address to the server's fully qualified DNS name.

If you decide not to use a central directory service, you need to set up the same users and groups in the Accounts pane of System Preferences on each SAN computer.

> **NOTE** ▶ If you create users and groups on each SAN computer, be sure of the following:
>
> ▶ Each user or group has a numeric user ID (UID) or group ID (GID) that is unique throughout the SAN.
>
> ▶ Each user or group defined on more than one computer has the same UID or GID on each computer.

Configuring Xsan Volumes

Many factors must be considered when deciding how best to configure your storage. The topics below will help you to focus your attention on those areas that will have the most impact on your decision making.

Choosing Storage Capacity

Because it's easy to add user data storage to an Xsan SAN, you initially need only to select an adequate starting point. You can add storage later as needed, up to a maximum of 2 petabytes.

However, you can't expand a storage pool that can store only volume metadata and journal data, so right at the start you should allocate enough space for metadata. (You can add an entire storage pool for metadata and journal storage.)

Note that the number of RAID systems you use affects not only available space but also SAN performance. See "Optimizing Performance," in this chapter.

Displaying Available Storage

If you want the users working on a specific project to see a volume dedicated to their work, create a separate volume for each project. If it's acceptable for a user to see a folder for his or her work on a volume with other users' folders, you can create a single volume and organize it into project folders.

Managing Workflow

How much file sharing is required by your users' workflow? If, for example, different users or groups work on the same files, simultaneously or in sequence, it makes sense to store those files on a single volume to avoid the need to maintain or hand off file copies. Xsan uses file locking to manage shared access to a single copy of a file.

Optimizing Performance

If your SAN supports an application that requires the fastest possible sustained data transfers (such as high-resolution video capture and playback), design your SAN with these performance considerations in mind:

▶ Set up the LUNs (RAID arrays) using a RAID level that offers high performance. See "Choosing RAID Levels for LUNs," later in this chapter.

▶ Assign your fastest LUNs to an affinity tag for the application. Assign slower LUNs to an affinity tag for less demanding applications.

▶ To increase parallelism, spread LUNs across several RAID controllers. Xsan will stripe data across the LUNs, and it benefits from simultaneous transfers through two RAID controllers.

▶ To increase parallelism for an affinity tag assigned to relatively small LUNs (the size of one or a few drive modules), create a slice of similar size across all the drives on a RAID controller instead of creating the LUNs from just one or two drive modules.

▶ Spread file transfers across as many drives and RAID controllers as possible.

▶ Try creating slices across the drives in RAID systems, and then assign these slices to the same affinity tag.

▶ To increase throughput, connect both ports on client Fibre Channel cards to the fabric.

▶ Store file system metadata and journal data on a storage pool separate from user data, and make sure that the metadata LUNs are not on the same RAID controller as any user data LUNs.

▶ Use a second Ethernet network (accessed through a second Ethernet port in each SAN computer) for the SAN metadata; or, at least, use a router to isolate the SAN's Ethernet network SAN from the company intranet or the Internet.

▶ If your SAN uses directory services, mail services, or other services on a separate server, connect SAN computers to that server on an Ethernet network that is separate from the SAN metadata network.

▶ Choose a different primary metadata controller for each volume, and set up volume failover priorities to minimize the possibility of more than one volume failing over to the same metadata controller.

Setting the Controller-to-LUN Ratio

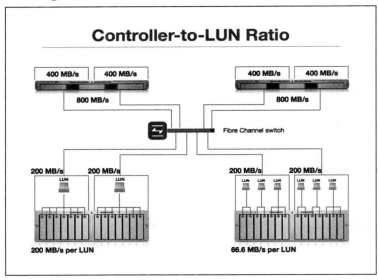

A single LUN that is associated with a single controller with a maximum bandwidth of 200 MB/s will be able to access all the available bandwidth for data. However, if that controller has three LUNs associated with it, the 200 MB/s bandwidth will be divided three ways, resulting in a throughput of 66.6 MB/s per LUN. Therefore, given the maximum bandwidth of the controller, it is simple math to compute how many LUNs can be assigned to that controller before sufficient bandwidth is no longer available for each LUN.

Evaluating Availability

If high availability is important for your data, set up at least one standby metadata controller in addition to your primary metadata controller. Also, consider setting up dual Fibre Channel connections between each client, metadata controller, and storage device using redundant Fibre Channel switches.

> **NOTE ▶** Be warned that losing a metadata controller without a standby can result in the loss of all data on a volume. A standby controller is highly recommended.

Enforcing Security

If your SAN will support projects that need to be completely secure and isolated, you can create separate volumes for each secure project to eliminate the possibility of the wrong client or user accessing files stored on the volume.

As the SAN administrator, you control which client computers access each volume. Clients can't browse for or mount SAN volumes on their own. Use Xsan Admin to unmount a volume on clients that shouldn't have access to it.

You can also set up access control lists (ACL) in Xsan Admin or assign user and group permissions to folders using standard file-access permissions in the Finder.

Choosing RAID Levels for LUNs

Much of the reliability and recoverability of data on a SAN is not provided by Xsan, but by the RAID arrays you combine to create storage pools and volumes. Before you set up a SAN, use the RAID system configuration or administration application to prepare LUNs based on specific RAID schemes.

> **NOTE ▶** Be warned that if a LUN belonging to an Xsan volume fails and can't be recovered, all data on the volume is lost. It is strongly recommended that you use only redundant LUNs (LUNs based on RAID schemes other than RAID 0) to create Xsan volumes.

LUNs configured as RAID 0 arrays (striping only) or LUNs based on single drives are difficult or impossible to recover if they fail. Unprotected LUNs such as these should be used only for volumes that contain scratch files or other data that you can afford to lose.

Most RAID systems support all popular RAID levels. Each RAID level offers a different balance of performance, data protection, and storage efficiency, as summarized in the following table.

LUN RAID Levels

RAID level	Minimum number of drives required	Storage efficiency	Read performance	Write performance	Data redundancy
RAID 0	2	Highest	Very high	Highest	No
RAID 1	2	Low	High	Medium	Yes
RAID 3	3	High to very high	Medium	Medium	Yes
RAID 5	3	High to very high	High	High	Yes
RAID 6	4	Medium to high	High	High	Yes, very

RAID is a system of combining multiple hard drives for sharing or replicating data among those drives. The benefits of RAID are increased capacity, data integrity, fault tolerance, and performance.

Xsan doesn't provide any reliability or redundancy beyond what you get with RAID redundancy. In other words, you gain reliability from the RAID sets that you choose, not from the way your SAN volumes are configured. Choosing reliable RAID sets is very important. Because of the way data is striped on the LUNs that make up the volume, the failure of a single LUN results in the loss of all data on that volume. For this reason, a non-redundant RAID scheme such as RAID 0 should be avoided. If you must use RAID 0, you should move it to a separate Xsan volume entirely, so that its failure won't affect other storage pools. RAID 0 might make sense for a scratch disk, for example.

Ultimately, the type of RAID scheme you choose for your LUNs will be determined by a combination of factors that includes the following:

▶ The number of drives in your setup

▶ Your requirements for read performance

▶ Your requirements for write performance

▶ Your requirements for data redundancy

When these requirements have been defined, you will be able to choose an appropriate RAID scheme.

Redundant RAID arrays allow data to be read or written even if there is a hardware fault. The redundancy in mirrored data or parity allows the RAID controller to access the duplicate copy or to regenerate the data using the parity information.

Redundancy is provided by duplicate hardware (RAID 1) or by parity (RAID 3 or RAID 5). Striping (RAID 1) has the highest hardware costs. Parity-based RAID has lower hardware costs and also usually has lower performance on writes.

RAID types vary according to performance, hardware cost, and redundancy.

▶ **RAID 0: Striping.** RAID 0 distributes data evenly in horizontal stripes across an array of drives. While RAID 0 offers substantial speed enhancements, it provides no data protection. If one drive fails, all of its data is lost and all drives must be reformatted. RAID 0 provides the most efficient use of drive capacity because no storage space is dedicated to redundant data or parity information.

▶ **RAID 1: Mirroring.** RAID 1 creates a pair of mirrored drives with exactly the same data. It provides a high level of data availability and, by using both drives simultaneously, offers fast read performance. Write speeds are lower, however, because all data is written twice—once to each drive. RAID 1 is also relatively expensive to deploy because it offers the poorest level of drive efficiency and storage capacity.

▶ **RAID 3: Striping.** RAID 3 stripes data across two or more drives and stores parity data on a dedicated drive. In the event of a disk failure, the redundant parity bits can be used to reconstruct data on any drive. RAID 3 offers fast read rates and high data availability, along with greater storage efficiency than RAID 1. Write performance in

RAID 3 is faster than RAID 1, but not as fast as RAID 5, because it depends on the availability of a separate parity drive. RAID 3 requires a minimum of three drives, but using more drives results in faster performance and greater drive efficiency.

▶ **RAID 5: Striping with distributed parity.** RAID 5 distributes data and parity information across an array of drives one block at a time, with each drive operating independently. This enables maximum read performance when accessing large files and improves performance in a transaction-processing environment. Write performance is also improved because parity information is striped across the drives, removing the bottleneck of a single parity drive. RAID 5 is the most popular configuration for high-throughput protected storage. Like RAID 3, RAID 5 requires a minimum of three drives. Using more drives provides faster performance and higher storage efficiency. If a single drive in a RAID 5 LUN fails, the data would be reconstructed from the parity data striped across the other hard drive in that LUN.

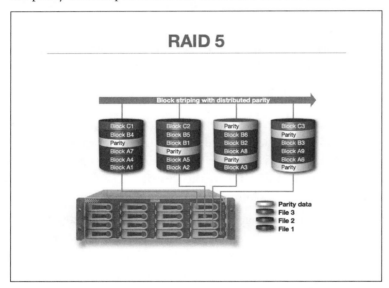

▶ **RAID 0+1: Striping over mirroring.** This hybrid RAID level is created by striping data across multiple pairs of mirrored drives. With Xserve RAID, both striping and mirroring are set up in hardware, which means the array can run independent of the server processor. RAID 0+1 provides higher throughput with simpler setup than protected configurations that use software RAID for striping, such as RAID 10.

▶ **Additional RAID levels.** Additional RAID schemes, such as RAID 10, 30, and 50, use a combination of hardware RAID and software striping. In a DAS environment, you would use a tool such as Disk Utility to implement the software striping across two or more RAID 1, RAID 3, or RAID 5 sets. Xsan supports its own striping mechanism to achieve similar results, so you won't deal directly with these RAID levels when using Xsan.

Selecting RAID Levels for Xsan

RAID 1 (mirroring) can provide slightly better performance than Xsan's default RAID 5 scheme for the small, two-drive metadata LUNs that Xsan uses to store volume information. A single drive is almost always adequate for storing the primary volume metadata (10 GB of metadata space is enough to serve approximately 10 million files). The second, mirror drive protects you against metadata loss. If one drive should fail, the second drive would still function and contains all of the original data.

Both the Xserve RAID and Promise VTrak RAID systems are optimized for excellent performance and data redundancy using a RAID 5 scheme. Some RAID systems ship configured as RAID 5 LUNs. RAID 0 (striping with no parity) might give slightly better write performance but provides no data-recovery protection, so RAID 5 is always a better choice for LUNs that store user data.

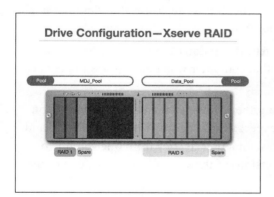

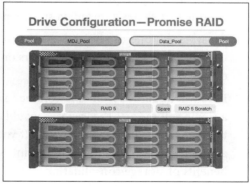

For LUNs that store metadata and journaling information, a RAID 1 scheme is recommended because it provides a level of redundancy for that critical data. When using Xserve RAIDs for metadata and journaling, it is ideal to have this LUN managed by a dedicated RAID controller configured with a hot spare drive that can provide protection in the event of a drive failure. When using a Promise VTrak E-Class RAID, it is not necessary to dedicate a controller for metadata and journaling in most instances. However, if your bandwidth requirements are greater than 70 percent of the throughput of the controller that manages your metadata and journal LUN, you should consider dedicating a controller to that LUN.

Choosing the Number of Volumes

A volume is the largest unit of shared storage on the SAN. If your users need shared access to files, you should store those files on the same volume. This makes it unnecessary for them to pass copies of the files among themselves.

Affinities can be used to ensure that specific files are stored on specific storage pools. However, creating a separate volume would give you the same level of control over which LUNs are used for a given operation. For example, if you had two applications that would work best with a specific block allocation size, you would create a separate volume for each application. Each volume would be optimized for the particular disk activity of the users.

Keep the following factors in mind when considering affinities versus volumes:

▶ Each volume needs its own metadata storage pool. You can create affinities on a single volume that shares a metadata storage pool.

▶ Separate volumes can be mounted separately. If you don't mount the Video volume on a given client, non-administrators on that computer won't have access to the data on the volume.

▶ Files will be copied from one volume to another. Moving a file between affinities on a single volume acts the way you would expect a move to act: It is instantaneous, and the file is moved instead of copied. If you want a user to copy from one volume to another, you may end up with multiple versions of the same file, negating one of the benefits of storage consolidation.

On the other hand, if security is critical, you can control client access by creating separate volumes and unmounting volumes on clients that shouldn't have access. Be careful not to rely on this technique too heavily as a security measure. If a user has administrator access to a client computer and knows the volume name, he can mount the volume manually using a command-line mount command.

For a more typical balance of security and shared access, a flexible compromise is to create a single volume and control access with folder access privileges or access control lists in Xsan Admin (or in Mac OS X Server's Server Admin).

Organizing a Volume

You can help users organize data on a volume or restrict users to specific areas of the volume by creating predefined folders. You can control access to these folders by assigning access permissions using Xsan Admin.

You may want to assign folders to specific storage pools using affinities. For example, you could create a folder for data that requires fast access and assign that folder to your fastest storage pool.

If you create multiple volumes, decide which volumes should be mounted on which clients. A new volume is mounted initially on all clients. You can use Xsan Admin to unmount a volume from selected clients.

Choosing Metadata Controllers

When deciding how best to configure the SAN and the SAN volume, it is important to think about the metadata controllers and how those controllers will be configured.

Selecting Primary and Standby Metadata Controllers

You must identify at least one computer to be the SAN metadata controller, the computer that is responsible for managing file system metadata.

> **NOTE** ▶ File system metadata and journal data are stored on the SAN volume, not on the metadata controller.

If you have a small number of clients or if high performance is not critical, you can use a single computer as both the client and metadata controllers. You can even set up a SAN consisting of a single storage device and a single computer that acts as both controller and client (to provide network attached storage, for example).

If high availability is important, you should use at least two metadata controllers, one as the primary controller and one as a standby. You can specify additional metadata controllers as needed, and set each volume's failover priorities to determine the order in which the controllers are tried if a volume's primary controller stops responding.

When performance is critical, don't run other server services on the metadata controller and don't use the controller to reshare a SAN volume using AFP or NFS.

To be sure that SAN volumes are always available, set up at least one standby metadata controller that can take over if your primary metadata controller fails. In most cases this machine will be identical in configuration to the primary controller. This is especially true if the primary controller is hosting multiple volumes.

Combining Clients and Controllers

A single computer can function as both a metadata controller and a client. It's possible, for example, to set up a SAN consisting of a single RAID system and one computer that acts as both controller and client. Any computer you specify as a controller can also act as a client.

If, for example, you don't have a computer to dedicate as a standby metadata controller, you can assign a computer that is normally used as a client to take over controller duties if the primary metadata controller fails.

Choosing the Volume Configuration

When choosing the volume configuration for your SAN, you should keep in mind that each preset volume type has its own requirements and is recommended for different uses.

Assigning LUNs to Affinity Tags

When you create a volume using a preset volume type that fits your SAN scenario, Xsan Admin automatically sets up storage pools and affinity tags for best performance. All you do is assign LUNs to each affinity tag. Xsan Admin determines the optimal number of storage pools to create, based on the volume type and the number of LUNs you assign to each affinity tag. For best performance, you should assign LUNs in the multiples shown in the following table. These multiples apply to affinity tags used for user data, not to the Metadata and Journal affinity tag, which needs just one LUN.

Type	LUN multiples	Storage pool names
HD Video	4	Video Audio Other
SD Video	4	Video Audio Other
2K and 4K Video	4	Video Audio Other
General File Server	2	Data
Home Folder Server	2	Home
Mail Cluster	1	Mail
Podcast Producer Cluster	1	Calendar
Final Cut Server	4	Video Audio Other
Custom		

You should assign LUNs that have the capacity and performance characteristics similar to each affinity tag.

LUNs that you assign to an affinity tag should have the same capacity because Xsan provides high performance by using the RAID 0 scheme to stripe data across the LUNs in each storage pool. This striping scheme can use available space on each LUN that is equal to the capacity of the smallest LUN in a storage pool. If a storage pool's LUNs vary in size, this can result in wasted capacity. For example, if a storage pool has a 240 GB RAID array and a 360 GB RAID array, 120 GB of the larger array will not be used. By assigning LUNs with similar capacities to an affinity tag, you avoid wasting available storage.

If you're using a volume type with multiple affinity tags for user data, assign your fastest LUNs to the affinity tag that will be associated with folders whose contents will benefit most from extra performance. Assign slower LUNs to an affinity tag that will be associated with folders whose contents don't require critical performance.

You can also increase the performance of an affinity tag's storage pools by assigning that affinity tag a combination of LUNs hosted on different drive modules and different RAID controllers. This strategy increases performance by increasing the parallelism of data transfers.

Choosing Where to Store Metadata and Journaling Data

The metadata and journal data that describe a volume are not stored on the volume's metadata controller but on the volume itself. By default, they are stored on the first storage pool in the volume.

All preset volume types set up a separate storage pool used only for metadata and journal data. For best performance, make sure that the LUNs you assign to the metadata and journal storage pool are connected to a different RAID controller than the LUNs that you assign to affinity tags for user data.

If you set up a custom volume with more than one storage pool, you can choose which storage pool is used to store metadata and journal data. You may get adequate performance by combining metadata and journal data on the same storage pool as user data; but for better performance, use a separate storage pool for metadata and journal data.

Choosing an Allocation Strategy

Your allocation strategy governs the order in which data is written to the storage pools that make up a volume. If only a single storage pool is present in the SAN, the allocation strategy is irrelevant. If you choose a preset volume type when you set up a volume, Xsan Admin sets a volume allocation strategy for you. Later, you can change the allocation strategy by editing volume settings using Xsan Admin. The allocation strategy you choose for a volume determines the order in which its storage pools are filled with data. You can choose *round robin*, *fill*, or *balance*.

If you choose round robin, Xsan writes new data to each storage pool in the volume in turn. This is normally the best choice for performance.

If you choose fill, Xsan writes all new data to the first storage pool in the volume until that storage pool is full, and then moves to the next storage pool. This is a good choice if you want to keep a particular storage pool unused as long as possible.

If you choose balance, Xsan writes new data to the storage pool with the most free space.

Choosing the Stripe Breadth

Xsan uses both the storage pool stripe breadth and the volume block allocation size to decide how to write data to a volume. For most SANs, the default values result in good performance. However, in some cases you may improve read and write performance by adjusting these values to suit a specific application.

The stripe breadth of a storage pool is the number of file allocation blocks that are written to a LUN in the pool before moving to the next LUN. To choose an efficient stripe breadth, you need to consider three factors:

▶ The Mac OS X and Mac OS X Server 1 MB data transfer size

▶ The number of LUNs in the storage pool

▶ The size of the data blocks written and read by the critical application that uses the volume (as reflected in the block allocation size for the volume)

▶ Knowing these values, choose a stripe breadth using this formula:

```
stripe breadth = (transfer size / number of LUNs) / block allocation size
```

where stripe breadth is expressed in blocks, and transfer size and block allocation size are expressed in bytes.

For example, if you use an application such as Final Cut Pro to move large amounts of video data to and from a storage pool consisting of four LUNs, choose a block allocation size of 256 kilobytes and use the equation to find the stripe breadth of 1 block. Then, Xsan will write 256 KB of data, in turn, to each LUN in your video storage pool.

The stripe breadth must be set when the volume is created; it can't be changed for an existing volume.

Choosing the Block Allocation Size

The block allocation size is the smallest number of bytes that can be reserved on, written to, or read from an Xsan volume. Xsan uses the volume block allocation size together with the storage pool stripe breadth to decide how to write data to a volume. If you create a volume based on a built-in volume type (for example, General File Server or Calendar Server Cluster), Xsan Admin automatically sets optimum values. For most volumes, the preset block allocation size and storage pool stripe breadth result in good performance. However, in some cases you may be able to improve read or write performance by adjusting these settings to suit a specific application. Thus, if your application reads and writes small blocks of data, you might improve performance by choosing a correspondingly small block allocation size.

For example, if your application reads and writes 16 KB blocks of data, you can try adjusting the block allocation size to 16 KB and then calculate a corresponding stripe breadth for the volume's storage pools using the same formula as above.

If four LUNs are in the volume's data storage pools, the calculation becomes

```
stripe breadth = (1048576 / 4) / 16384
```

This gives a stripe breadth of 16.

Choosing the Number of Storage Pools

There are two primary reasons to have multiple storage pools:

▶ To store your metadata and journal data on a separate storage pool from your user data. The benefit is that the full bandwidth of the data pool is available for user data. If you store the metadata on the same storage pool as user data, your clients share the same bandwidth with the metadata controller.

▶ To configure more than one storage pool in a volume. You can take advantage of different performance or reliability characteristics of different storage pools. You've seen how you can use block size, stripe breadth, and the number of LUNs to make a storage pool optimized for a specific application. What if you have two types of applications for your SAN? Capturing audio and capturing video may have far different bandwidth requirements. You can create two storage pools, each tuned to its individual needs, and still store them on the same Xsan volume. You can then use affinities to mark the storage pools with descriptive folder names, such as Audio and Video.

Affinities are a way to force particular files to a particular storage pool in a volume. In the absence of affinities, storage space in a volume is allocated according to the volume allocation strategy, which defines how multiple storage pools are utilized within a volume.

If you have multiple storage pools that use the same affinity tag, you will get the best performance for that affinity group by choosing the round robin allocation strategy. For example, if you have eight data LUNs and are building a SAN volume for video, you would get more throughput to all of the clients by creating two storage pools instead of creating a single large pool.

What You've Learned

▶ What system specifications are required of clients of an Xsan 2 SAN.

▶ What components are required to deploy a Fibre Channel network.

▶ What the Ethernet network requirements are for an Xsan 2 deployment as well as the distance limits and fiber-connector compatibilities.

▶ All client systems on the SAN will attempt to resolve the IP address on their private metadata interface. To alleviate this, it is best to provide fully qualified domain names (FQDN) for all IP addresses, public and private, on the SAN.

▶ A Network Time Server is critical for keeping logs and file information synchronized. In general, having a local Network Time Server internally on your own network will lead to machines syncing faster, syncing more reliably, and being in tighter sync than using an external NTP server for all the hosts on your internal network.

▶ If your SAN doesn't have access to an existing directory service, you can specify during initial setup of your Xsan primary metadata controller that you want to use Xsan Admin to manage your users and groups. The setup assistant creates an Open Directory master server on your primary metadata controller and sets up Open Directory replica servers on your standby metadata controllers.

▶ Xserve RAID and Promise VTrak are the only storage systems qualified by Apple to work with Xsan and the characteristics of those storage systems.

▶ A number of volume types are preset in Xsan Admin, and they have different performance characteristics and requirements.

▶ Many things must be considered when designing the storage configuration of an Xsan 2 volume.

References

Administration Guides

Mac OS X Server: Network Services Administration for Version 10.5 Leopard, Second Edition (http://images.apple.com/server/macosx/docs/Network_Services_Admin_v10.5_2nd_Ed.pdf)

Mac OS X Server: Open Directory Administration for Version 10.5 Leopard, Third Edition (http://images.apple.com/server/macosx/docs/Open_Directory_Admin_v10.5_3rd_Ed.pdf)

Mac OS X Server: User Management for Version 10.5 Leopard
(http://images.apple.com/server/macosx/docs/User_Management_v10.5.mnl.pdf)

VTrak E-Class/J-Class Quick Start Guide, Version 1.0, Firmware 3.29
(www.promise.com/apple/Apple_VTrak_E-J-Class_%20QSG_v1.0_final.pdf)

VTrak E-Class Product Manual, Version 2.0
(www.promise.com/apple/VTrak_E-Class_PM_v2.pdf)

Xsan 2 Setup Guide
(http://images.apple.com/xsan/docs/Xsan_2_Setup_Guide.pdf)

Xsan 2 Administrator's Guide
(http://images.apple.com/xsan/docs/Xsan_2_Admin_Guide.pdf)

Apple Knowledge Base Documents
"Promise VTrak: Configuring for optimal performance"
(http://support.apple.com/kb/HT1200)

"Xsan 2: Integrating Promise VTrak RAIDs into an existing Xsan 2 deployment"
(http://support.apple.com/kb/HT1110)

"Xsan: Synchronizing clocks is important"
(http://support.apple.com/kb/TA25097)

"Fibre Channel Hardware Compatibility Guide"
(http://support.apple.com/kb/HT1769)

Review Questions

1. Identify the system requirements for Promise Storage with Xsan 2.
2. What factors should you consider when specifying a Fibre Channel switch?
3. What is the maximum cable run length from a client to an Ethernet switch?
4. When purchasing fiber optic connectors, why should you make sure that they are qualified for use in a Fibre Channel network?
5. If a controller on a Promise VTrak fails, what happens to the LUNs associated with that controller?

6. Why is a network time server recommended for Xsan deployments?

7. How does the deployment of Directory Services assist with user and group management?

8. Why is it undesirable to associate multiple LUNs with more than one RAID controller?

Answers

1. When using Promise VTrak storage with Xsan 2, your system must be configured with an Intel processor and either Mac OS X v10.5.2 or Mac OS X Server v10.5.2.

2. Port Density, Expandability, Speed, Management, and Power.

3. 100 meters.

4. Fiber optic connectors for both Ethernet and Fibre Channel look the same. However, they support different protocols. For example, Cisco SFPs for Ethernet networks look identical to Finisar SFPs used for Fibre Channel. Only the protocols supported are different.

5. The second controller in the RAID takes over the management of those LUNs until the first controller is replaced.

6. Having all clients bound to the same network time server helps to synchronize files and processes that rely on date or time stamps.

7. Directory Services allows for the centralization of user and group management.

8. This was true with the Xserve RAID but is not necessarily true with the Promise RAID. The more LUNs associated with a controller, the lower the bandwidth available to each LUN. On an Xserve RAID, multiple LUNs on a controller could have a serious impact on the performance of that LUN and storage pool. However, with the Promise VTrak, the performance of the controller has four times the amount of bandwidth available on an Xserve RAID controller. Therefore, the number of LUNs per controller is not as critical.

3

Time   This chapter takes approximately 6 hours to complete.

Goals   Configure Ethernet and Fibre Channel infrastructure for a SAN

          Configure SAN storage for use with Xsan

          Configure Xsan clients and servers

          Set up a new SAN

          Create a shared volume

          Understand the eight preset deployment options available in Xsan 2

          Identify the function of Volume Affinities during the initial volume
          configuration in Xsan Admin

Chapter **3**
Deployment

This chapter explains how to connect SAN networks, configure a Fibre Channel switch, configure Network Services, configure Xsan clients and servers, prepare RAID arrays (LUNs), use the Xsan Admin application, set up a new SAN, and create a shared volume.

Building upon the knowledge you gained in the previous two chapters and the SAN strategy you've developed, you should have a clear plan for how your SAN will go together and how the volume will be configured.

In this chapter, you'll apply those plans to the deployment of a real-world SAN. You will make decisions for your SAN and SAN volume related to:

- ▶ Ethernet network design
- ▶ Network Services you will deploy
- ▶ Directory services
- ▶ Fibre Channel network design
- ▶ Storage configuration
- ▶ Client and server configuration
- ▶ SAN and SAN Volume configuration

Configuring Ethernet Networks

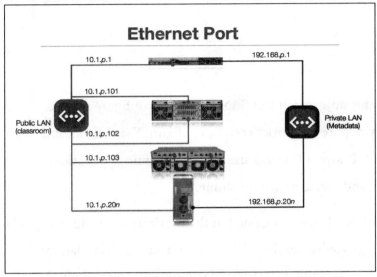

As it is best practice to deploy a separate Ethernet network for metadata, the first step is to configure the public Ethernet network, and then configure the private metadata network.

1 Place both the public and private Ethernet switches in their permanent locations.

2 Turn on the public Ethernet switch and connect it to the main network or to an outbound router.

3 Connect the first Ethernet port on each SAN computer to the public Ethernet switch.

4 Connect the Ethernet ports on each RAID storage system to the public Ethernet switch.

5 Connect the Ethernet port on each Fibre Channel switch to the public Ethernet switch.

6 For any non-SAN client that will be managing the SAN, connect its Ethernet port to the public Ethernet switch.

7   Turn on the private metadata Ethernet switch. (You should connect this switch only to SAN clients or other private metadata Ethernet switches. Do not connect this switch to the public Ethernet network.)

8   For each SAN computer, use an Ethernet cable to connect the second Ethernet port to the private metadata Ethernet switch.

Setting Up Network Services

With the public and private metadata Ethernet networks in place, you may configure the network services to be used by SAN clients.

It is recommended (but not required) that you do not run the network services described here on a SAN client. This allows the SAN to be brought down when required, without affecting the other services provided to SAN clients.

A DNS and Network Time server are required for Xsan 2 to perform optimally, whereas mail services are optional. If your deployment requires that status notification be sent outside of the local network, a mail server will be needed to do so.

Configuring a DNS Server

A DNS is critical to a successful Xsan deployment. If you do not have access to a DNS server, you can configure one on a Mac OS X v10.5.2 Server system.

To configure a DNS Server:

1   Open Server Admin and connect to the server.

2   Click Settings.

3   Click Services.

4   Select the DNS checkbox.

5   Click Save.

6   In the list of Services, choose the DNS Service.

7 Click Zones.

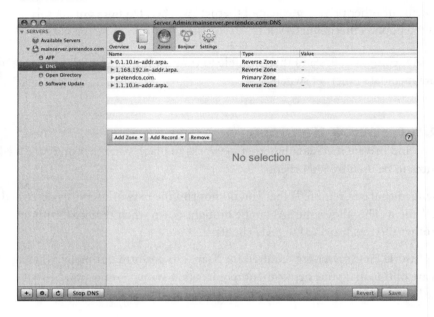

8 Click Add Zone, and choose "Add Primary Zone (Master)."

9 Select the new zone (example.com.).

10 In the Primary Zone Name field, enter the zone name.

This is the fully qualified domain name of the primary server.

11 Enter the mail address of the zone's administrator.

12 Select "Allows zone transfer" to permit secondary zones to get copies of the primary zone data.

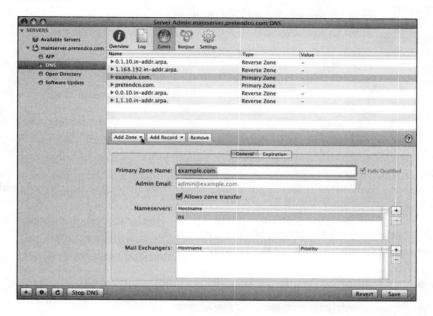

13 Double-click the "ns" Nameserver and type the name of your Nameserver.

14 From the "Add Record" pop-up menu, choose "Add Machine."

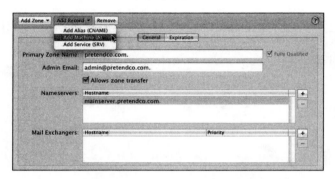

15 Click the new machine listed under the primary zone, and in the Machine Name field, enter the host name of the computer.

This field is the basis for the A record of the computer. Reverse lookup Pointer records are automatically created for the computer.

16 Click the Add (+) button, and enter the IP address of the computer.

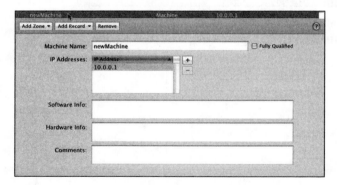

17 Repeat steps 14 through 16 until you have entered the DNS information for all devices on your SAN.

18 Click Save.

19 In the list of Services, choose the DNS Service.

20 Near the bottom of the pane, click the Start DNS button.

Your server has now been configured to provide DNS to your SAN and any other computers on your network.

For additional information on DNS configuration, you can consult the *Network Services Administration* guide at the Mac OS X Server Resources page (http://images.apple.com/server/macosx/resources).

Running a Network Time Server

If you decide to run NTP service on your network, make sure your designated NTP server can access a higher-authority time server. Apple provides a Stratum 2 time server for customer use at http://time.apple.com.

Make sure that your firewall permits both NTP queries to an authoritative time server on UDP port 123 and incoming queries from local clients on the same port.

To set up the NTP service, do the following:

1 Open Server Admin and connect to the server.

2 Click Settings; then click Date & Time.

3 Select "Set date & time automatically."

4 From the pop-up menu, choose the server you want to act as a time server.

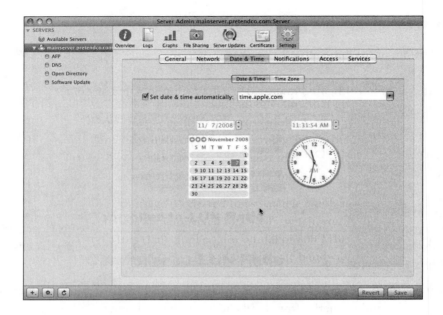

5 Click General.

6 Select the "Network Time Server (NTP)" checkbox.

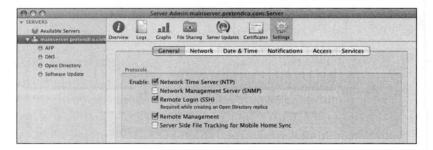

7 Click Save.

Setting Up Directory Services

In many deployments, directory services are the glue that holds together the entire workflow. With Xsan 2, you can choose how you enable directory services. You can set Xsan Admin to configure directory services on the Primary Metadata Controller, or you can set up a separate Open Directory master and bind all of your systems to that server. In the next exercise, you'll focus on building a separate Open Directory master.

To configure a separate Open Directory master:

1   Open Server Admin and connect to the server.

2   Click the triangle to the left of the server.

The list of services appears.

3   From the expanded Servers list, choose Open Directory.

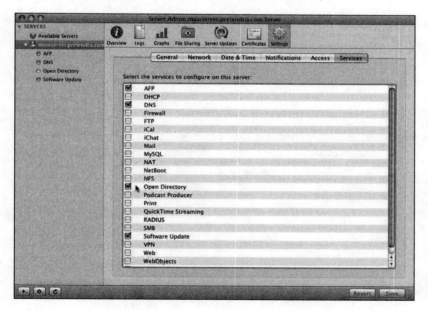

4   Click Settings; then click General.

5 Click Change.

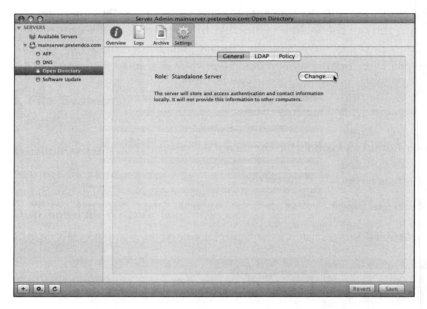

This opens the Service Configuration Assistant.

6 Choose Open Directory Master; then click Continue.

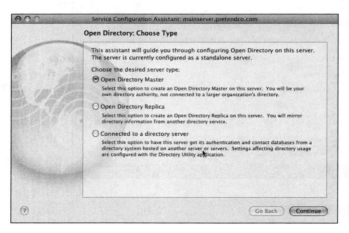

At this point, you must create a user account for the primary administrator of the LDAP directory. This account is not a copy of the administrator account in the server's local directory domain. The names and user IDs of the LDAP directory administrator should be different from the names and user IDs of user accounts in the local directory domain. If you want to prevent the directory administrator account from being listed in the login window, you should assign the directory administrator account a user ID below 100. Accounts with user IDs below 100 are not listed in the login window

7   Enter the Master Domain Administrator information for Name, Short Name, User ID, and Password. Click Continue.

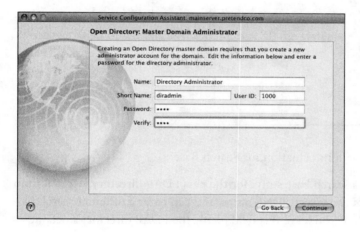

8   Enter the Master Domain information for Kerberos Realm.

This field is preset to be the same as the server's DNS name, converted to capital letters. This is the convention for naming a Kerberos realm. You can enter a different
name, if necessary.

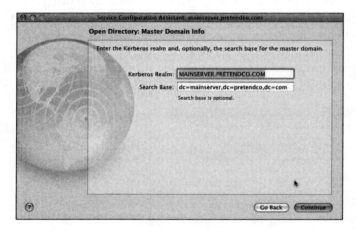

9   Enter the Master Domain information for Search Base.

This field is preset to a search base suffix for the new LDAP directory, derived from
the domain portion of the server's DNS name. You can enter a different search base
suffix or leave it blank. If you leave this field blank, the LDAP directory's default
search base suffix is used.

10 Click Continue.

11 Confirm your settings; then click Close.

12 Confirm that the Open Directory master is functioning properly by clicking Overview (near the top of the Server Admin window, with Open Directory selected in the Servers list).

The status of all items listed in the Open Directory overview pan should say "Running."

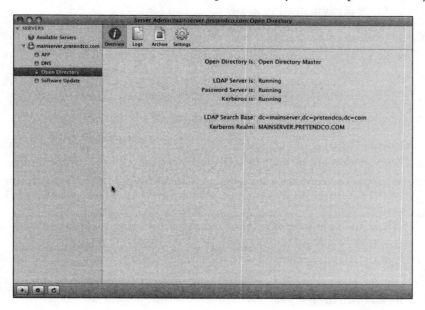

Now that you have a functioning Open Directory master, it is time to add users and groups to the directory.

Creating Users and Groups

Because the setup wizard for Xsan 2 will guide you step-by-step through the creation of users and groups, the next exercises will quickly explore the basics of creating users and groups using Workgroup Manager. For more detailed information on user and group creation, see the Mac OS X Server documentation suite.

To create a user or group account in a directory domain, you must have administrator privileges for that domain. If you created the Open Directory master in the previous exercise, you can use those directory domain administrator credentials to access the directory.

A group account stores the identities of users who belong to the group, along with information that enables you to customize the working environment for members of that group. When you define preferences for a group, the group becomes a *workgroup*.

A *primary group* is a user's default group. Primary groups can expedite the validation performed by the Mac OS X file system when a user accesses a file.

When you want multiple users or groups to have the same file permissions, or when you want to apply the same management settings to all users or groups, add the users or groups to a group.

After assigning a user to a primary group, you don't need to add the user to that group. However, you must specifically add users to other groups.

You can use Workgroup Manager to add a user to a group if the user and group accounts are in an Open Directory domain or the local directory domain. Although some group information doesn't apply to Windows users, you can also add Windows users to groups that you create.

Mac OS X Server v10.5 and later supports *hierarchical groups*—groups composed of nested groups. When preferences for a parent group are managed, child groups also receive these managed preferences.

Creating a User Account

In this exercise, you'll use Workgroup Manager to create a user account.

1   In Workgroup Manager, click Accounts.

2   Verify that the directory services of the Mac OS X Server computer you are using are configured to access the directory domain.

3   Click the globe icon and choose the domain where you want to locate the user's account.

For Mac OS X Server v10.5 or later, local and /local/Default refer to the local directory domain.

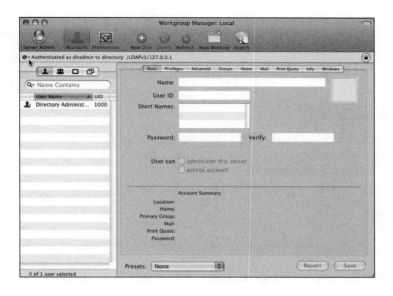

4   To authenticate, click the lock icon and enter the name and password of a directory domain administrator.

5   Choose Server > New User or click New User in the toolbar.

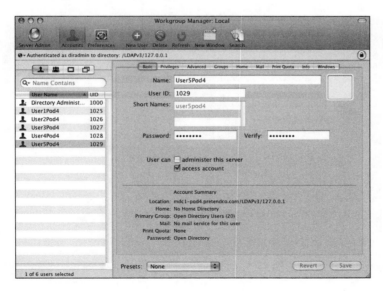

6 In the panes provided, specify settings for the user.

After the account has been created, you can continue adding users or move on to creating group accounts.

Creating a Group Account

With user accounts in place, use Workgroup Manager to create a group account.

1 In Workgroup Manager, click Accounts.

Make sure the directory services of the Mac OS X Server computer you are using are configured to access the directory domain.

2 Click the globe icon and choose the domain where you want to locate the group's account.

3 To authenticate, click the lock, and enter the name and password of a directory domain administrator.

4 Click the Groups button.

5 Click New Group and specify settings for the group in the appropriate fields.

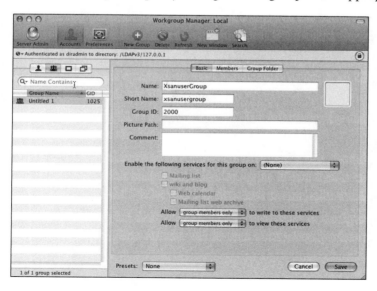

6 Click Save.

After the group account has been created, you can continue creating group accounts or move on to adding users to the group accounts.

Adding a User to a Group Account

In this exercise, you'll add users to the group account.

1   In Workgroup Manager, click Accounts.

2   Choose the group you want to modify.

3   To select an account, click the globe icon and choose the directory domain where the account is located.

4   Click the Groups button, and select the group.

5   To authenticate, click the lock icon, and enter the name and password of a directory domain administrator.

6   In the Members pane, click the Add (+) button to open a drawer that lists the users and groups defined in the current directory domain.

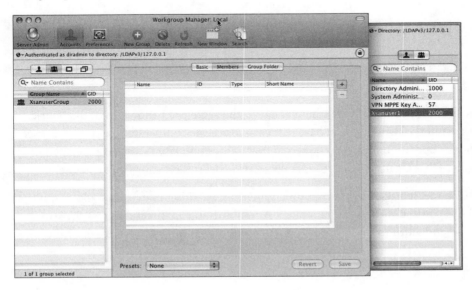

7   Select the user account, drag the user into the list, and click Save.

You should create as many of the user and group accounts as possible before you set up the SAN volume and begin assigning permissions and/or quotas. Doing so makes the management of the SAN much easier and more efficient.

Configuring a Fibre Channel Network

After all of the fiber for your deployment has been installed and tested, you can install and configure your Fibre Channel switches.

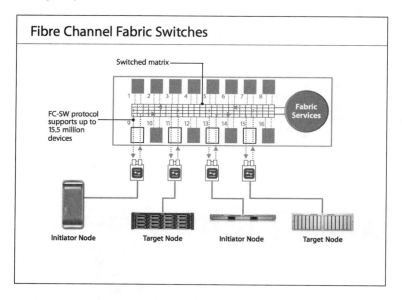

As devices are added to a Fibre Channel fabric, the aggregate bandwidth of that fabric increases and the switches must have sufficient aggregate bandwidth to handle full-speed, full-duplex operation on every connected port. Therefore, Fibre switches should be used instead of Fibre Channel hubs for interconnecting devices on your Fibre Channel network.

Fibre Channel fabric switches contain an internal switching matrix that allows multiple devices to communicate simultaneously. A nonblocking architecture gives the switch the internal bandwidth to route frames concurrently across multiple data paths. All of the nodes connected to a switch can transmit and receive at full speed (200 MB/s over 2 Gb Fibre Channel and 400 MB/s over 4 Gb Fibre Channel). This is often referred to as *scalable bandwidth*. For example, if two targets and two initiators are connected to a 4 Gb switch, you could have two concurrent transactions at 400 MB/s (half-duplex) for a total bandwidth of 800 MB/s. If 16 devices were connected to the same 4 Gb switch, the aggregate bandwidth would be 6400 MB/s.

Choosing a Fibre Channel Switch

A number of Fibre Channel switches are qualified by Apple for use with Xsan. These include switches from Brocade, Cisco, and QLogic. The QLogic SANbox product line is the most popular Fibre Channel switch for Xsan deployments. As such, a little time will be spent on some basic configuration information on the 5000 series SANbox switch.

QLogic provides a configuration and management tool called QLogic Enterprise Fabric Suite 2007, but it requires specific firmware, and so on. The QuickTool Java Web tool from QLogic is used for the following exercises.

When used with Xsan, the basic configuration of the QLogic 5000 series switch includes the configuration of:

▶ Administrator account preferences (password)

▶ Network interface

▶ I/O Stream Guard (RSCN)

▶ Device Scan

▶ Zoning (optional)

Before you can configure the final three items listed, you must make sure that *all* SAN storage and *all* SAN clients are turned on and cabled correctly. If not, you will not see the WWPN (WorldWide Port Name) in the management window and will not be able to configure I/O Stream Guard or Device Scan, or to assign the equipment to specific zones. To confirm or modify each of these configurations, use the following procedures.

Connecting to a Fibre Channel switch

The current iteration of the QuickTool is not compatible with Safari; therefore, the Firefox browser should be used to connect to and configure the switches in this exercise.

1   Open Firefox and connect to the IP of your switch.

If this is the first time you are connecting to this switch and it is brand new, the IP address is 10.0.0.1.

2   If a window appears verifying the authenticity of the signature's certificate, click Trust.

The Add a New Fabric dialog appears.

3   Enter the admin user name and password for the switch, and click Add Fabric.

If this is the first time you are connecting to this switch or you have not changed the admin password, use the default user name and password for the switch. The default user name is *admin* and the default password is *password*.

4   If a non-secure connection warning appears, dismiss it by clicking Yes.

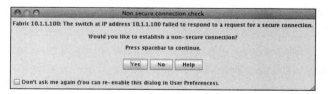

Configuring Administrator Account Preferences

Now that you are connected to your switch, the first thing to do is to change the password for the admin user.

1   Choose Switch > User Accounts.

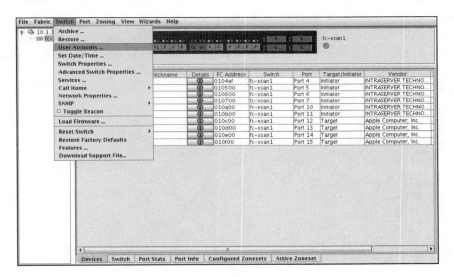

2   When the User Account Administration pane appears, select the admin user and, near the bottom of the pane, click the Change Password tab.

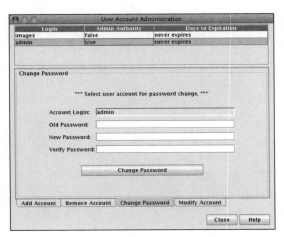

3 After you have changed the password fields, click the Change Password button.

4 After the changes are made and your browser updates, click Close.

Configuring a Network Interface

Now that the admin password is changed and your switch is secure, you can change the switch's IP address information. It is a good idea to also have a fully qualified domain associated with the switch so that you can manage it without needing to remember the IP address.

1 Choose Switch > Network Properties.

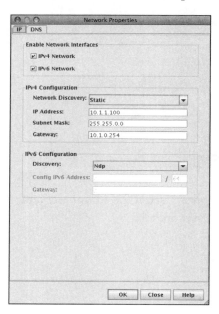

2   In the Network Properties dialog, enter the new IP address, Subnet Mask, and
    Gateway information for the switch.

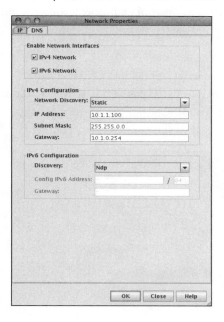

3   Click OK.

    If you changed the IP address of the switch, you will need to reconnect to the new IP
    address with Firefox.

Configuring I/O Stream Guard and Device Scan

At any moment in time, a Fibre Channel fabric is very dynamic in terms of the number
and state of the component connections. Because of this, the Fibre Channel protocol
allows devices, typically initiators, to register their ports with the switch's name server to
receive notifications of changes in the state of the fabric. Changes in the state of the fabric
can occur when devices enter or leave it, such as when a device's power is cycled.

In certain real-time deployments, such as video environments, these state-change notifications can disrupt the flow of data on the fabric and, in extreme cases, result in dropped
frames. As a result, in video deployments, it is common practice to suppress these notifications on initiator ports.

If your initiators are nodes in a high-performance computing cluster, they may rely on RSCN (Registered State Change Notification) for proper functionality. RSCN suppression is called different things by different vendors. Some vendors don't support it directly and, instead, require the creation of separate zones within a switch to isolate initiators from one another.

I/O Stream Guard (QLogic's RSCN-suppression feature) prevents Fibre Channel fabric disruption by suppressing the communication of RSCNs. But if your initiators are nodes in a high-performance computing cluster, they may rely on RSCNs for proper functionality. Refer to your switch documentation for appropriate settings in your own environment.

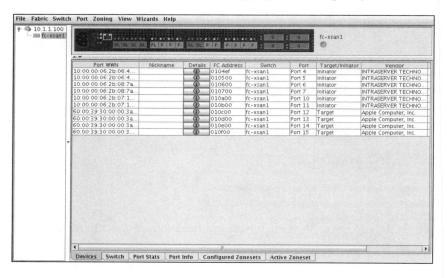

The preceding figure displays all of the switch ports and indicates which ports have devices attached, as well as showing the devices' World Wide Node (WWN) addresses and device type (initiator or target). The WWN and WWPN are both assigned to a device during the manufacturing process and cannot be changed. Remember, initiators are the clients and controllers on the SAN while targets are the storage.

To configure I/O Stream Guard and Device Scan:

1   Verify which ports are connected to initiators. If you know some machines are missing, make sure they are turned on and connected to the switch via Fiber.

2 Command-click the icon of each port that is an initiator.

3 Choose Port > Port Properties.

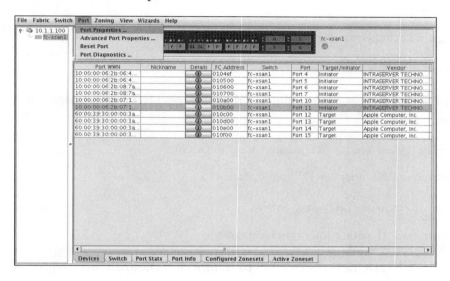

The Port Properties dialog appears.

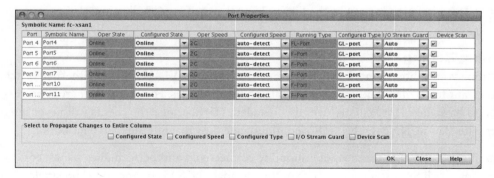

4 For each of the initiator ports, change I/O Stream Guard from Auto to Enable.

5   Deselect the Device Scan checkbox for all initiator ports.

6   Click OK.

The switch will make the changes and provide you with a status update.

7   Click OK.

8   Command-click the icon for each port that is a target.

9   Choose Port > Port Properties.

10   In the Propagate section at the bottom of the pane, select I/O Stream Guard and Device Scan.

11   For one of the entries, set I/O Stream Guard to Disable.

The settings in the other rows should update.

12   Select Device Scan for one of the entries.

The settings for the other rows should update.

13   Click OK to dismiss the Port Properties pane; then click OK to dismiss the Port Properties dialog.

14   Close Firefox to log out of the Fibre Channel switch Java application.

Using Zoning

Zoning your Fibre Channel switch is similar to creating a VLAN on your Ethernet switch. You want to segment and control the traffic between nodes. For example, there is no reason to have the client systems "see" the metadata LUN because the clients will never interact with that LUN. Only the MDCs communicate directly with the metadata LUN.

Zoning can also help when troubleshooting connectivity and performance issues. For example, if all SAN storage (other than the metadata LUN) is in one zone and single clients are also in their own zone, you could set up another zone for each client in which only the specific client and storage can "see" each other. In this scenario, none of the other client systems have any knowledge of the other SAN clients. Should an issue with the fiber connection on one client become problematic, the connection is much easier to trace.

Zoning the Fibre Channel switch is optional for the majority of installations. However, if you determine that zoning is required, an example of the process by Aaron Freimark can be viewed at the Xsanity website (www.xsanity.com). Search for *Bulletproof Zoning on Xsan.*

Note that the zoning of a QLogic 9000 series switch is *not* optional. If you are deploying a QLogic 9000 series switch, you must configure an o*rphan zone.* Orphan zones are configured by default on QLogic 5000 series switches.

Before you can configure your switch for zoning, you need to ensure that all of your systems (storage and clients) appear in the Devices pane. If they do not, you should verify that their physical connections are working properly. If you are still not able to see all of the clients and you are running Mac OS X v10.5 with an Apple Fibre Channel PCI-X card, open the Fibre Channel preferences in System Preferences and confirm that the topology is set to Point to Point for both ports. If the topology is not set to Point to Point, change that setting, and then reboot the system.

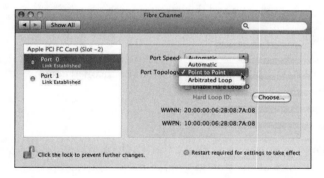

Notice that Fibre Channel preferences also show both the WWNN and WWPN for each port on the Apple Fibre Channel HBA. Whether you have launched this preference from Mac OS X v10.5 Server or client, you will see the same information. This information is important when implementing zoning on your fabric, as you will need to identify each of your clients and its ports when you are configuring the switch. Take note of this information to save a lot of time later.

Setting Up the Storage Devices

Integrating a Promise RAID into a SAN that includes Xserve RAIDs can be tricky. Promise VTrak is significantly faster and has much greater bandwidth than the Xserve RAID. Generally, accepted best practice is to not mix and match Xserve RAIDs with Promise RAIDs in the same storage pools. Some deployments have used Xserve RAIDs for metadata and kept the Promise RAIDs for user data, with varying success.

By now, you should have decided how storage should be configured and the storage options that you have available. Specifically, you need to be concerned with the RAID levels used for the LUNs in an Xsan volume, the management configurations of the storage, the process for creating the LUNs, and the performance tuning options.

Choosing RAID Levels for Xsan

RAID 1 and RAID 5 are the most popular RAID levels for Xsan. RAID 1 is the recommended level for metadata LUNs as the mirrored drives provide a high level of data availability and fast read performance. If a single drive in the mirror fails, the RAID continues to function until a replacement drive is initialized. However, RAID 1 is also relatively expensive to deploy because it offers the poorest drive efficiency and the lowest storage capacity.

For most applications, storage pools that contain user data should have LUNs that are initialized with a RAID 5 scheme. Using more drives provides faster performance and higher storage efficiency. If a single drive in a RAID 5 LUN fails, the data can be reconstructed from the parity data striped across the other hard drive in that LUN.

Selecting Controller-to-LUN Ratio

Because the data in a SAN is written and read from LUNs by a storage pool, you should create your LUNs with the total performance of the storage pool in mind. For example, if you know that your application is going to require 320 MB/s data rates, you'll need to have at least a single storage pool capable of that read/write rate. If the controllers on your RAIDs are capable of providing 80 MB/s of bandwidth, you know that you will need four controllers per storage pool. However, if you cut the performance by allocating more than one LUN per controller, you will need to have more controllers per storage pool. The theoretical bandwidth of the storage pool is the throughput per controller multiplied by the number of controllers assigned to that storage pool.

These performance considerations are especially critical in a video or high-bandwidth environment. Of course, the performance and configuration will differ depending upon your storage configuration. If you are using Xserve RAIDs in this type of environment, you will get the highest aggregate bandwidth by setting up an Xsan volume with multiple storage pools of four LUNs each, with each LUN on its own RAID controller. If you are building a video SAN with Promise VTrak RAIDs and JBODs, you will get the best performance with an Xsan volume by using the available scripts from Apple for the volume type that you implement. Nonetheless, you should still test the performance by using the actual applications that will be writing data to the SAN.

Using Xserve RAID

The RAID Admin application is used to configure and manage the Xserve RAID.

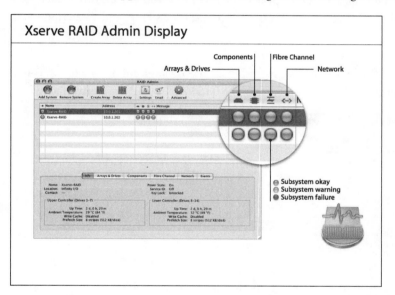

RAID Admin is a cross-platform Java-based tool for creating storage volumes, managing preferences, and monitoring storage hardware on Apple's Xserve RAID storage device. The utility reports information about all Xserve RAID systems on the network, using green, yellow, and red icons to indicate the health of each subsystem. It allows administrators to easily monitor detailed information about the status and performance of each component. If operating conditions for any subsystem exceed predefined thresholds, the Xserve RAID controller can automatically notify the administrators via email, pager, or email-capable cell phone, allowing them to stay in touch with storage deployments and resolve issues without downtime or data loss.

Using RAID Admin, you can view the system name, lock status, controller details, and problems and power failures as they occur. You can view detailed information about each array and its drives available and in use, as well as the power supplies, RAID controllers, cooling modules, and cache backup batteries.

RAID Admin also provides information about each RAID controller, including its IP address, and related network details, along with the type of Fibre Channel connection in use.

Events that have occurred for both RAID controllers are listed in chronological order. Each event has a color symbol indicating the severity of the event, a time stamp, and a description.

Creating a LUN

To create a LUN in Xserve RAID Admin, you will select the RAID level, choose the drives you want in the LUN, and specify whether to initialize in the background and use a drive cache.

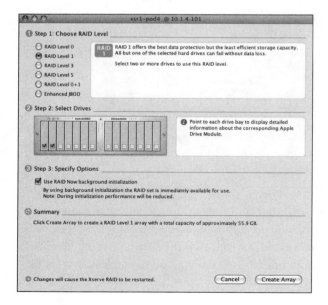

On the Xserve RAID, an unassigned drive is *hot* (always spinning and ready for use) and available to any array on its controller. A hot spare drive reduces the available storage of the controller, but requires no human intervention in the event of a failed drive.

The Xserve RAID architecture also supports hot-swappable media. If no hot spares are available in the event of a drive failure, the failed drive can be replaced without turning off the Xserve RAID. The RAID controller automatically detects the new drive and begins repairing the RAID set automatically.

A spare drive is used automatically by the RAID controller for its group of drives whenever a drive within an array fails. A controller can only use available drives on its side of the system; it cannot treat a drive on the other side as a hot spare.

Tuning RAID Performance

RAID system performance settings, which affect parameters such as drive caching, RAID controller caching, and read prefetching, can have a significant effect on Xsan volume performance. Follow these guidelines:

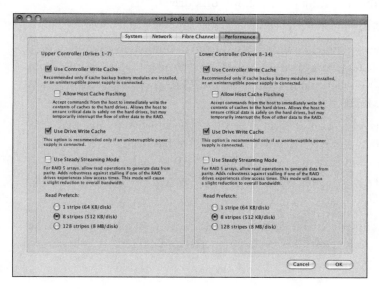

▶ Enable Drive Write Caching.

In addition to the caching performed by the RAID controller, each drive in an array can perform its own caching at the drive level to improve performance.

NOTE ▶ Be warned that if you enable drive caching for a RAID set, the system must be connected to an uninterrupted power supply (UPS). Otherwise, you could lose cached data if the power fails.

▶ Enable RAID Controller Write Caching.

Without RAID controller write caching, a request to write data to the associated LUN is not considered finished until the data has been completely written to the physical disks that make up the array. Only then can the next write request be processed. (This is sometimes called *write-through caching*.)

When RAID controller write caching is enabled, a request to write data is considered finished as soon as the data is in the cache. This is sometimes called *write-back caching*. Write requests are processed more quickly because the file system can write to the fast cache memory without waiting for the slower disk drives.

Be sure to enable write caching on RAID controllers that support metadata storage pools.

Although some large write requests might benefit from caching, they often do not. By placing a volume's metadata storage pool on a RAID controller that is separate from the data storage pools, you can enable caching on the RAID metadata controller, and disable caching on the RAID data controller.

When the file system is relying on caching in this way, you must guarantee that data in the cache isn't lost before it is written to disk. Data that has been written to disk is safe if the power fails, but data in a cache is not. To be sure that a power failure won't cause the loss of cached data, protect your RAID systems with RAID controller backup batteries or a UPS.

NOTE ▶ Be warned that if you enable controller write caching on a RAID system, be sure that the system includes controller backup batteries and, preferably, is connected to a UPS.

▶ Enable Read Prefetching.

Read prefetching is a technique that improves file system read performance when data is read sequentially, as in the case of audio or video streaming. When read prefetching is enabled, the RAID controller assumes that a read request for a particular block of data will be followed by requests for subsequent, adjacent data blocks. To prepare for these requests, the RAID controller not only reads the requested data, but it also reads the following data and stores it in cache memory. Then, if the data is requested, it is retrieved from the fast cache instead of from the slower disk drives.

Using Promise VTrak

The VTrak E-Class RAID can be managed through a command line interface or command line utility using an RJ-11 Serial Port, Telnet, or the WebPAM PROe web tool supplied with the RAID. The VTrak RAID comes with an embedded web server and management support that does not require a special host agent. For information on using tools other than WebPAM PROe, consult the Promise VTrak user guide.

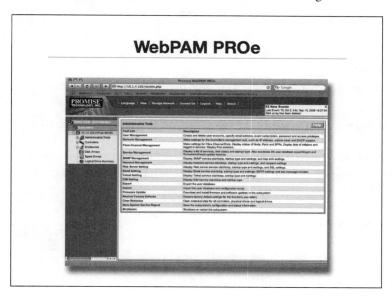

The WebPAM PROe web-based management tool allows the management and configuration of VTrak E-Class RAID features, such as storage, subsystem configuration files, and configuration files.

You must change the VTrak's default network settings so that the VTrak can function properly on your network. In most cases, you can use WebPAM PROe to make the appropriate change.

The table below lists the default VTrak network settings:

Component	Default Setting
Virtual Management Port IP address	10.0.0.1
RAID Controller 1 IP address	10.0.0.2
RAID Controller 2 IP address	10.0.0.3
Subnet Mask	255.0.0.0
DHCP Support	Disabled
User Name	Administrator
Password	password

Connecting with VTrak

To establish an Ethernet connection between your Mac and the VTrak:

1 Be sure that each controller is connected to the network and the RAID is powered on.

2 On your Mac, go to Network Preferences and temporarily set the Network address to 10.0.0.10 (you can use any number from 4 to 254 after the last dot) and the Subnet to 255.0.0.0.

3 On your Mac Desktop, open Safari.

4 In the address field, type *http://10.0.0.1/* and press Return.

   The log-in page appears.

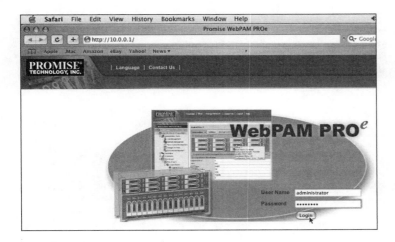

5   In the User Name field, type *administrator*.

6   In the Password field, type *password*.

NOTE ▶ The user name and password are case sensitive.

7   Click Login.

Changing VTrak Settings

To change the VTrak's network settings:

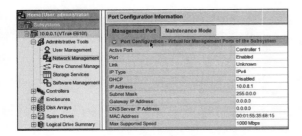

1   Next to the Administrative Tools, click the Add (+) button.

2   Click the Network Management icon.

3   In the Management Port tab, click the Port Configuration link.

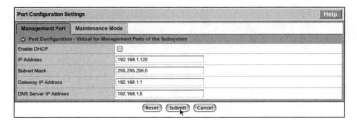

4   Type the settings you desire into the IP Address, Subnet Mask, Gateway IP Address, and DNS Server IP Address fields.

5   Click Submit.

> **NOTE** ► When your VTrak is fully configured, you should make the same network settings for the individual RAID controllers.

Restarting VTrak

Now that you have made changes to the network settings of the RAID, you need to restart the system. To restart the VTrak:

1   Click the Administrative Tools.

2   Click the Shutdown link.

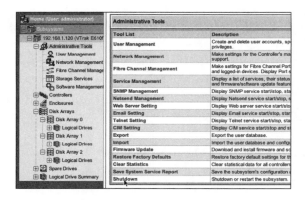

In the Shutdown dialog, be sure *restart* is chosen in the Option menu.

3   Click Submit.

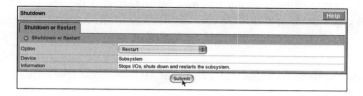

The confirmation dialog appears.

4   In the confirmation box, type *confirm*.

5   Click OK.

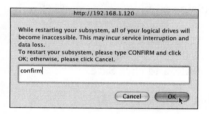

6   In the WebPAM PROe header, click Logout to log out of WebPAM PRO. Wait a few minutes for the VTrak to reboot.

7   On your Mac, go to your Network preferences and restore the original settings.

Choosing a LUN Configuration Script

Creating LUNs on the Promise VTrak is a multistep process that begins with the preparation of the configuration scripts and culminates with confirmation that the scripts prepared the LUNs as desired.

Preparing a Configuration Script

Go to the article "Promise VTrak: Configuring for optimal performance" (http://support.apple.com/kb/HT1200) to select the best script for your deployment. The scripts are listed under "Configure via script."

1   Carefully read the descriptions and choose the script that matches your application. Click a script name to choose it.

2   Highlight the entire script from *#Begin Copy* through *#End Copy*; then press Command-C to copy it.

3   Open TextEdit and press Command-V to paste the script into a new file.

    Be sure to convert the configuration script to a plain text file.

4   Choose Format > Make Plain Text.

5   Choose File > Save As. Type a name for the script file, and click Save.

    Your configuration script is ready to import using WebPAM PROe.

Importing a LUN Configuration Script

A configuration script works only when all of your physical drives are unconfigured. If you are setting up your VTrak system for the first time, all of your drives will be unconfigured. So you should start the script-importing process by checking your physical drives.

1   If WebPAM PROe is not running, open Safari and log in to WebPAM PROe.

2   In the tree view, choose VTrak > Enclosures > Enclosure > Physical Drives.

    In the Information tab, look at the Operational Status and Configuration Status of each physical drive. If the Operational Status is OK and the Configuration is Unconfigured, your physical drives are ready to run the configuration script.

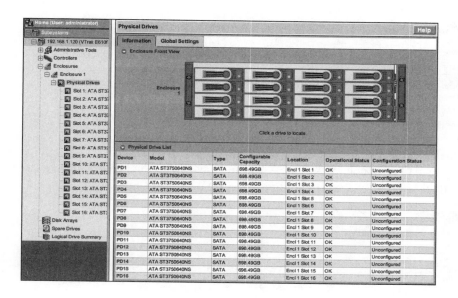

If you have created any disk arrays, logical drives, or spare drives, you must delete them before you run the script. Be sure you first back up your important data; then you can delete the disk arrays and logical drives. For further instructions, see the VTrak E-Class Product (User) Manual. After confirming that all drives are unconfigured and operational, you're ready to upload and run the configuration script.

3   In the tree view, click Administrative Tools, and click the Import link.

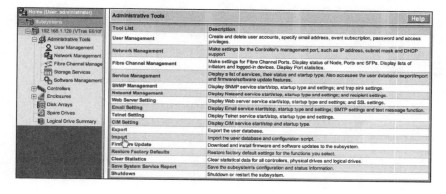

4   In the Import File dialog, in the Type pop-up menu, choose Configuration Script.

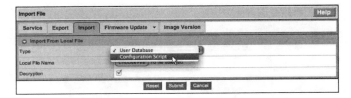

5   In the Import File dialog, click Choose File and navigate to the folder where you saved the configuration file. Select the configuration file and click Choose.

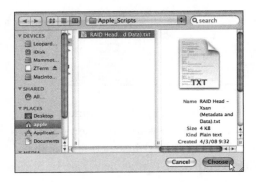

6   In the Import File dialog, click Submit.

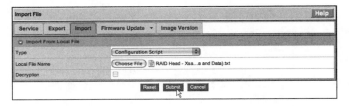

7 In the Import File dialog, click Next.

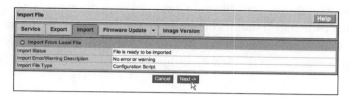

A warning dialog appears.

8 Click OK.

The configuration script takes about 30 to 45 seconds to upload and run. When the script is done, new disk arrays and logical drives appear in tree view. The exact appearance of the tree view will depend on how you set up your system and which script you chose.

Your VTrak system is now configured and ready to use.

9 In tree view, click Logical Drives Summary to see the full representation of your new logical drives.

Tuning VTrak Performance

If you configured your VTrak with scripts available from Apple, your performance settings are already set and you have a system that is configured to get the best performance. However, if you configured your VTrak manually, you will need to ensure that you have the following configurations in place to get the best performance from your controllers and LUNs.

Configuring VTrak Controllers

For each controller, you will need to configure four separate settings: LUN Affinity, Adaptive Writeback Cache, Host Cache Flushing, and Forced Read Ahead.

1   Enable LUN Affinity.

VTrak subsystems with two controllers include a LUN Affinity feature. Normally, either controller can access all logical drives. LUN Affinity enables you to specify which controller can access each logical drive. Use this feature to balance the load of your logical drives between the two controllers.

To use LUN Affinity, you must have two controllers in the RAID and Enable LUN Affinity under the controller settings.

On the VTrak subsystem, you can set the logical drive write cache policy to Write Thru or Write Back.

2   Enable Adaptive Writeback Cache.

When you set the write cache policy to Write Back, your data is written first to the controller cache, and later to the logical drive. This action improves performance. To preserve the data in the cache in the event of a power failure, the subsystem must have a backup battery to power the cache.

The Adaptive Writeback Cache feature protects your data by changing the write cache settings while the cache backup battery is offline under the following conditions:

▶   The logical drive write policy is set to Write Back.

▶   The Adaptive Writeback Cache feature is enabled.

▶   The cache backup battery goes offline.

When these conditions are met, the write policy automatically changes to Write Thru. When the battery comes back online, the write policy automatically changes back to Write Back.

3 Disable Host Cache Flushing.

As with Xserve RAID, when this setting is enabled, the VTrak will accept commands from the host to immediately write cache contents to the hard drives. This allows the hosts to ensure that critical data is safely preserved, but may temporarily interrupt the flow of other data to the RAID.

4 Enable Forced Read Ahead.

Read Ahead anticipates the next read and performs it just before the request is made. This can result in increased performance. On the Xserve RAID, this is called *Read Prefetching*.

Configuring VTrak LUNs

The configurations for each of the LUNs in your RAID also need to be customized depending on whether each LUN will be a metadata LUN or a data LUN. However, there are some general configurations for LUNs regardless of the data they store:

▶ Xsan supports sector values of 512 bytes only.

▶ When creating disk arrays (LUNs), attempt to assign an equal number of hard drives to each controller module by alternating each LUN's Preferred Controller ID value between Controller 1 and Controller 2.

▶ All settings not specifically mentioned below should be left at their default values.

▶ The Stripe value remains set at 64K and the Sector value should remain set at 512 bytes.

When configuring a two-drive metadata LUN, you should configure the LUN accordingly:

1 Enable PDM (Predictive Data Migration).

Predictive Data Migration (PDM) is the migration of data from the suspect disk drive to a spare disk drive, similar to rebuilding a logical drive. But unlike rebuilding, PDM constantly monitors your disk drives and automatically copies data to a spare disk drive *before* the disk drive fails and your logical drive goes critical.

After the data is copied from the suspect disk drive, the controller marks it with a Stale configuration and a PFA error. Later, you can clear the Stale configuration and PFA error and put the disk drive back into service. In some cases, however, you might need to remove the disk drive for repair or replacement.

2   Enable Media Patrol.

Media Patrol is a routine maintenance procedure that checks the magnetic media on each disk drive. Media Patrol checks all physical drives assigned to disk arrays. It does not check unconfigured drives.

Media Patrol will also check spare drives if those drives have Media Patrol enabled. Media Patrol for spare drives is enabled by default. You can disable it in VTrak's command line interface.

Unlike Synchronization and Redundancy Check, Media Patrol is concerned with the condition of the media itself, not the data recorded on the media. If Media Patrol encounters a critical error, it triggers PDM, if PDM is enabled.

3   Set ReadPolicy to ReadCache.

4   Set WritePolicy to Write Thru.

When configuring more than three drives as a data LUN, you should configure the LUN accordingly:

1   Enable PDM.

2   Enable Media Patrol.

3   Set the ReadPolicy to Read Ahead.

4   Set the WritePolicy to Write Back.

Configuring Spare Drives

Now that you have configured all of the LUNs, you have to configure the spare drives.

1   Set the Spare Type to Global if the Spare Drive is available to all LUNs, or choose Dedicated if the Spare Drive is available to a specific LUN.

2   Select Revertible if you want data to migrate from the spare drive to a replacement drive. (Performance may be impacted during the migration procedure.)

3   Select the Physical Drive(s) to be configured as Spare Drives.

4   If the Spare Type is Dedicated, select the LUN to which the spare drive is dedicated.

Configuring Clients

Now that the Ethernet networks, Fibre Channel network, Network Services, Open Directory, and storage are configured, it is finally time to start working on the actual client workstations that will be using the SAN. You are not quite ready to configure the metadata controllers, but you're close.

In this exercise, you will visit each Mac OS X v10.5.2 client computer to set up the administrator account, configure network settings, and install the Xsan software.

> **NOTE** ▸ If you're configuring a client that is running Mac OS X v10.5.2 server, skip to the second set of steps.

Configuring a Client Computer

To configure a client computer, do the following:

1   Install any additional hardware you may need in the client computer. This could include additional RAM, a Fibre Channel card, a video card, and so on.

2   Turn on the client computer.

3   Follow the Mac setup assistant's onscreen instructions to set up the computer.

4 Enter the administrator account name and password that you plan to use. To simplify SAN setup, use the same administrator name and password on all computers in the SAN.

5 When the Mac setup assistant finishes and the Finder appears, open System Preferences.

6 Click Network preferences and choose the first Ethernet port, which should be connected to your public intranet and the Internet.

7 Choose to configure manually, and enter the static public IP address, subnet mask, router address, and DNS server for that client computer.

   Don't configure the port connected to the private metadata network—the Xsan setup assistant will configure it for you.

8 Open Date & Time preferences, and configure the computer to set the date and time automatically using a time server.

   All systems should use the same time server.

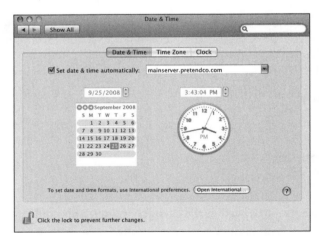

9 Close System Preferences and run Software Update.

10 Insert the Xsan installation disc. Double-click the Install Xsan.mpkg icon, and follow the onscreen instructions to install the Xsan software on the client computer.

11 When the process is completed, eject the Xsan installation disc.

12 Run Software Update again to verify that you have installed the latest version of Xsan 2.

13 If you configured an Open Directory master for this deployment, or already had one available, bind the client to Open Directory.

Configuring a Server as a Client

In some situations, the Xsan client will actually be a server running Mac OS X v10.5.2 server. For example, you may have file servers, Compressor clusters, Ingest systems, and so on. In that case, you should configure clients using the following steps:

1 Install any additional hardware the client computer may need. This includes additional RAM, a Fibre Channel card, a video card, and so on.

2 Turn on the client computer.

3 Follow the Mac OS X Server setup assistant's onscreen instructions to set up the computer. Pay special attention to the information in the following panes:

▶ Server Configuration: Select Advanced.

▶ Administrator Account: Enter the same account name and password used on your other clients as the Administrator Account.

▶ Network Address: If this pane appears, choose "No, configure network settings manually."

▶ Network Interfaces: Enable only the public Ethernet port. Disable the Ethernet port connected to the private metadata network—the Xsan setup assistant will configure it for you. If you are setting up an Intel-based Xserve, you can also enable the lights-out management port.

▶ TCP/IP Connection (public Ethernet port): Choose to configure manually and then enter the static public IP address, subnet mask, router address, and DNS server for the client computer.

▶ Time Zone: To ensure consistent time metadata across all computers in the SAN, choose a network time server for your client computers. All systems should use the same time server.

4 Run Software Update.

5 Insert the Xsan installation disc, double-click the Install Xsan.mpkg icon, and then follow the onscreen instructions to install the Xsan software on the client computer.

6 Run Software Update again to make sure you have installed the latest version of Xsan 2.

7 If you configured an Open Directory master for this deployment or already had one available, bind the client to Open Directory.

Configuring Metadata Controllers

The initial configuration of metadata controllers is similar to configuring clients. You will need to create the administrator account, set up the network preferences, and so on. However, this computer must have Mac OS X Server installed but not yet set up. You will configure the standby metadata controller first, and then configure the primary metadata controller.

Configuring the Secondary Metadata Controller

Follow these steps to configure the secondary or "backup" MDC (metadata controller):

1 Install any additional hardware the controller may need. This includes additional RAM, a Fibre Channel card, and so on.

2 Follow the Mac OS X Server setup assistant's onscreen instructions to configure the computer. Pay special attention to the settings in the following panes:

▶ Server Configuration: Select Xsan Metadata Controller.

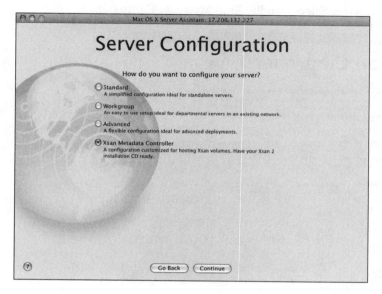

▶ Administrator Account: Enter the same account name and password that you used on all of your client computers.

▶ Network Address: If this pane appears, choose "No, configure network settings manually."

▶ Network Interfaces: Enable only the public Ethernet port. Disable the Ethernet port connected to the private metadata network—it will be detected and configured by the Xsan setup assistant. If you are setting up an Intel-based Xserve, you can also enable the lights-out management port.

▶ TCP/IP Connection (public Ethernet port): Choose the option to configure manually, and then enter the static public IP address, subnet mask, router address, and DNS server for the client computer.

▶   Time Zone: To ensure consistent time metadata across all computers in the SAN, choose a network time server for your client computers. All systems should use the same time server.

▶   Xsan Controller Type: Select Standby Xsan Metadata Controller.

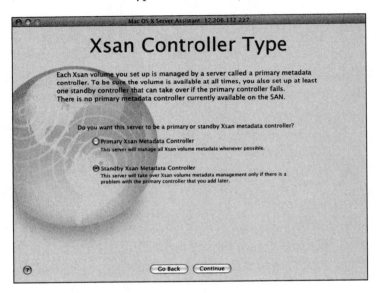

3   When prompted, insert the Xsan installation disc and follow the onscreen instructions to install Xsan.

4   Run Software Update.

5   If you configured an Open Directory master for this deployment or already had one available, bind the client to Open Directory.

The standby metadata controller is now ready to join the SAN and will be automatically detected by the primary metadata controller during SAN setup.

Configuring the Primary Metadata Controller

The last system to be configured is the primary metadata controller. When using Xsan 2 and Mac OS X v10.5 Server, the server assistant is Xsan aware and leads you through the installation and configuration of your SAN. You have waited until this stage to configure the primary metadata controller so that the entire process of bringing the SAN online will be automated. This computer must have Mac OS X Server v10.5.2 installed but not yet set up. To configure the primary metadata controller and SAN, follow these steps:

1   Install any additional hardware the controller may need. This includes additional RAM, a Fibre Channel card, and so on.

2   Follow the Mac OS X Server setup assistant's onscreen instructions to configure the computer. Pay special attention to the settings in the following panes:

▶   Server Configuration: Select Xsan Metadata Controller.

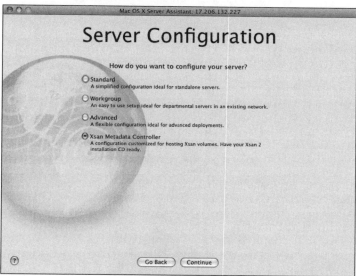

▶   Administrator Account: Enter the same account name and password that you used on all of your client computers.

▶ Network Address: If this pane appears, choose "No, configure network settings manually."

▶ Network Interfaces: Enable only the public Ethernet port. Disable the Ethernet port connected to the private metadata network—it will be detected and configured by the Xsan setup assistant. If you are setting up an Intel-based Xserve, you can also enable the lights-out management port.

▶ TCP/IP Connection (public Ethernet port): Choose the option to configure manually, and then enter the static public IP address, subnet mask, router address, and DNS server for the client computer.

▶ Time Zone: To ensure consistent time metadata across all computers in the SAN, choose a network time server for your client computers. All systems should use the same time server.

▶ Xsan Controller Type: Select Primary Xsan Metadata Controller.

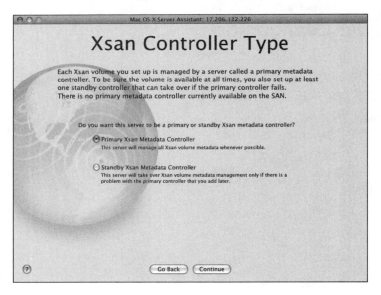

3   When configuring Users and Groups, for this exercise, you should choose "Manage users and groups with Xsan Admin." However, you are presented with three options:

▶   Manage users and groups with Xsan Admin: Select this option to have the server setup assistant create a centralized directory of users and groups on the primary metadata controller. Later, in the Add User Accounts pane, you have the option of creating some user accounts. The Mac OS X Server setup assistant creates the user accounts in the LDAP directory of the Open Directory server it creates on your primary metadata controller. After setup, you use Xsan Admin to create and delete users and groups and to change group membership.

NOTE ▶ You can select this option only while setting up Mac OS X v10.5.2 Server on the primary metadata controller. You can't configure this option after using the Mac OS X v10.5.2 Server setup assistant on the primary controller.

▶   Use existing users and groups from an Open Directory server: Select this option to have the Mac OS X Server setup assistant configure the primary metadata controller to connect to the Open Directory server whose DNS name or IP address you specify. If you select this option, Xsan Admin automatically configures all other SAN computers with Xsan 2 to use the Open Directory server.

If you need to set up an Open Directory domain, you can use Mac OS X Server's Server Admin application. Then, you can use the Workgroup Manager application to manage users and groups. For more information, see *Open Directory Administration* and *User Management* at the Apple Servers Resources page (www.apple.com/server/resources).

▶   Connect to a directory server later: Choose this option if you have another type of directory server, such as Active Directory.

4   After setting up the primary metadata controller, use the Directory Utility application on each SAN computer with Mac OS X v10.5 or Mac OS X v10.5 Server to connect the computer to your directory server. If you have client computers running Mac OS X v10.4.11 or Mac OS X Server v10.4.11, use the Directory Access application to connect these computers to the directory of users and groups.

5   If you choose not to use a directory service, you need to create the same set of users and groups in System Preferences on each SAN computer.

> **NOTE** ▶ If you create users and groups individually on each SAN computer, be sure that each user and group has a numeric user ID (UID) or group ID (GID) that is unique throughout the SAN, and all SAN users and groups have the same UID or GID on all SAN computers. One way to do this is to create an identical list of users and groups in the same order on each computer following a clean installation of the operating system.

▶   Add User Accounts: Choose "Add new user accounts now."

▶   Add New User Accounts: Enter a user name, short name, and password for each user who will log in to a client computer.

6   When prompted, insert the Xsan installation disc and follow the onscreen instructions to install Xsan.

7   When Xsan is installed, the Xsan setup assistant opens automatically.

At this point, you should close Xsan Admin and the SAN setup wizard. You will return to the SAN later in the chapter.

8   Run Software Update.

You have now configured all of your systems, and you're ready to build the SAN and the SAN Volume.

Creating the SAN and SAN Volume

In the previous exercises, Xsan Admin and the Xsan setup assistant started automatically after the basic server configuration completed. You closed Xsan Admin so that you could run Software Update before configuring the SAN. This allowed you to make sure everything was up-to-date. Now you will build the SAN and the SAN volume. Before beginning, you need to ensure that all of your clients, servers, Ethernet and Fibre Switches, as well as the storage, are turned on.

Configuring the SAN

You use Xsan Admin to configure the SAN. The first time you use Xsan Admin on a computer, it automatically starts the Xsan setup assistant.

You can use Xsan Admin on any computer with an intranet or Internet connection to your SAN computers. You can also use Xsan Admin on a computer that isn't connected to the SAN's private metadata network or its Fibre Channel network.

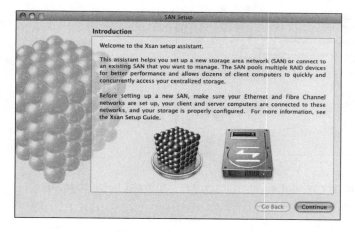

1   Open Xsan Admin (in /Applications/Server/).

2   In the Introduction pane, click Continue.

3   In the Initial SAN Setup pane, choose "Configure new SAN."

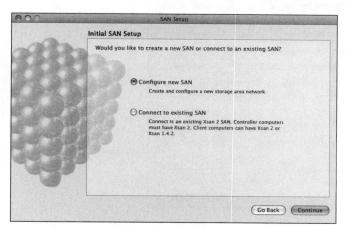

4   In the SAN Settings pane, in the SAN Name field, type a name for the SAN; and then, in the Administrator Name field, enter the SAN administrator's name, and in the Administrator Email field, enter his email address:

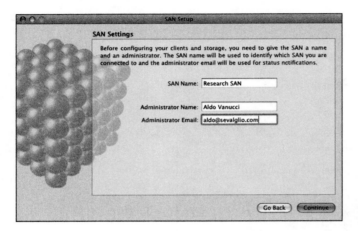

5   In the Add Computers pane, verify that all the computers you want to place in the SAN are selected.

If a computer you want to include isn't listed, make sure that you have installed Xsan on that computer, check that it is connected to both Ethernet networks, and verify the network settings in that computer's Network preferences.

NOTE ▶ You can also click Add Remote Computer to add computers manually.

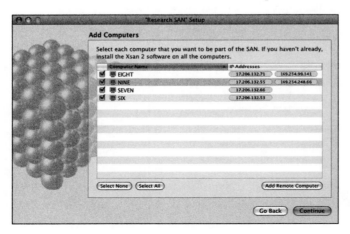

6 In the Authenticate SAN Computers pane, choose "Use same authentication information for all SAN computers," and in the User Name and Password fields, enter the user account name and password you entered on the clients and standby metadata controller.

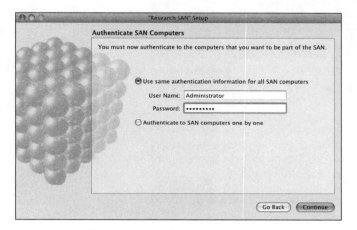

7 In the Serial Numbers pane, enter your Xsan serial numbers.

You can click Add Serial Number and type a number, or drag a text file to the list that contains the serial numbers.

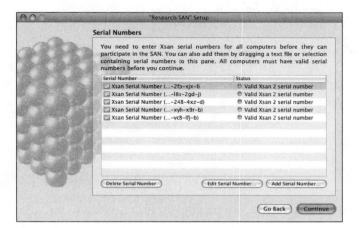

8 In the Choose Metadata Controllers pane, select only your primary and secondary metadata controllers. Deselect any client-only computers that appear.

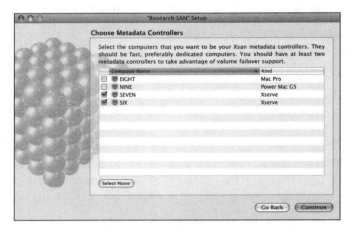

9 In the Private Metadata Network pane, choose "Yes, manage private Ethernet network settings."

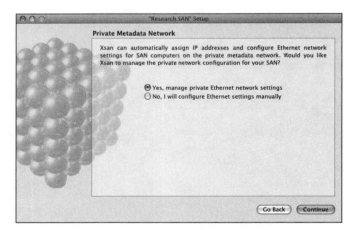

10 Review the Summary pane and, if all settings are correct, click Continue.

NOTE ► To change a setting, click Go Back until you reach the pane where you can correct the setting. Then click Continue until you return to the Summary pane.

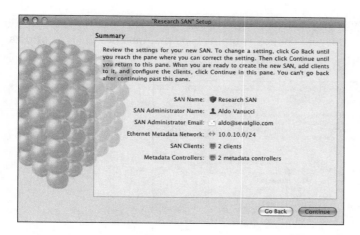

When the Xsan setup assistant finishes the basic SAN configuration, it asks if you want to set up a volume.

Configuring the SAN Volume

In the previous section, you just completed setting up the SAN. You will now configure the SAN volume.

1   In the Create Volume pane, choose "Create a volume now" and click Continue.

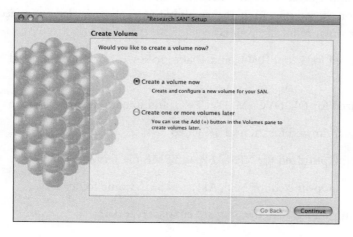

2   In the Volume Name and Type pane, in the Volume Name and Volume Type fields, type a name for the volume and choose a volume type that matches the type of data the volume will support.

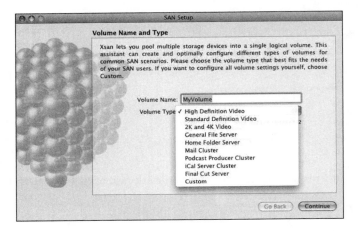

For the volume name, use only uppercase letters (A–Z), lowercase letters (a–z), numbers (0–9), and underscores (_). Don't include spaces or hyphens. The maximum length for a volume name is 70 characters.

The volume type you choose determines how the setup assistant will configure affinity tags and storage pools on the volume. Each of the volume types above is also optimized to provide the best performance for its given task:

▶ HD Video: Optimized for 720p, 1080p, and 1080i ProRes 422 or uncompressed HD video

▶ SD Video: Optimized for DV, DVCAM, DVCPRO, and uncompressed SD video

▶ 2K and 4K Video: Optimized for 2K and 4K video

▶ General File Server: Optimized for NFS, AFP, and SMB file servers

▶ Home Folder Server: Optimized for NFS, AFP, and SMB home folder servers

▶ Mail Cluster: Optimized for shared storage of email server data

▶ Podcast Producer Cluster: Optimized for Podcast Producer video and audio data

▶ iCal Server Cluster: Optimized for shared storage of calendar server data

▶ Final Cut Server: Optimized for shared storage of Final Cut Server data

▶ Custom: Advanced customization for expert users

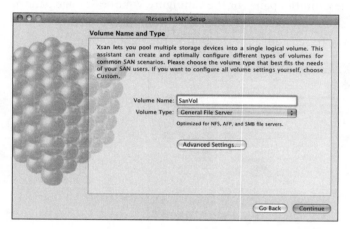

If you choose Advanced Settings, you can adjust the following volume settings.

▶ Block Allocation Size: If you're not sure what value to use, use the preset size.

▶ Allocation Strategy: Choose how storage for files is allocated among the storage pools that belong to the volume. If you choose Round Robin, each new request for space is assigned to the next available storage pool. If you choose Fill, all space is allocated on the first storage pool until it is full, then on the second storage pool, and so on. If you choose Balance, space is allocated on the storage pool that has the most free space.

▶ Spotlight: Enable this if you want Macintosh clients to search the contents of the volume using Spotlight.

▶ Access Control Lists: Leave this enabled if you want to use access control lists in Xsan Admin to control access to the volume and its contents.

▶ Windows ID Mapping: If you will have Windows clients on your SAN, choose how they map user and group information to the Xsan-compatible user IDs and group IDs they need in order to access this volume.

3   If the Label LUNs pane appears, choose "Automatically label all unlabeled LUNs with prefix" and click Continue. When the list of labeled LUNs appears, verify the LUN labels and click Continue.

4   In the Configure Volume Affinities pane (or the Configure Volume Storage pane, if you're configuring a custom volume type), drag LUNs from the left column to the corresponding affinity tag (or custom storage pool) in the right column.

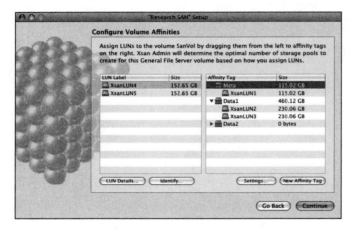

5   Drag the special metadata LUN you created earlier to the MetadataAndJournal affinity tag (or custom storage pool).

6   Drag your other LUNs to the other affinity tags (or storage pools).

    To avoid wasting storage, all LUNs assigned to an affinity tag (or storage pool) should be the same size.

7   When you finish, click Continue.

    You can select an affinity tag and click Settings to change the affinity tag name or other settings listed below. Affinities can be set up between a folder on the Xsan volume and a specific affinity tag. (After the Xsan volume is running and you have already assigned affinities to specific folders, you can create a folder with a different affinity in that main folder using the cvmkdir tool). If you're creating a custom volume, you can select it and click Storage Pool Settings to change the storage pool name or other settings:

▶ Affinity Tag (or Storage Pool Name): Type the name for the affinity tag (or custom storage pool). If the OK button is disabled when you finish typing the name, the name is reserved; try another.

▶ Use for: Choose the types of data that can be stored on storage pools that have this affinity tag (or that can be stored on the custom storage pool).

▶ Stripe Breadth: Specify how much data is written to or read from each LUN in storage pools that have this affinity tag (or each LUN in the custom storage pool) before moving to the next LUN. This value can affect performance. If you're not sure what value to use, use the preset value.

8 In the Volume Failover Priority pane, drag the controllers to reorganize the list, if necessary. The controller at the top of the list will be the primary controller. Click Continue.

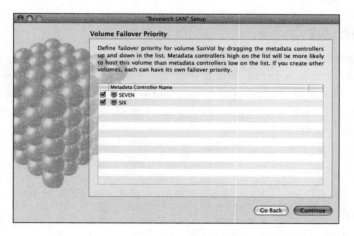

9 In the Setup Complete pane, click Continue.

Xsan Admin displays a summary of your SAN configuration, and the new volume is mounted and ready to use in the Finder on all clients and metadata controllers.

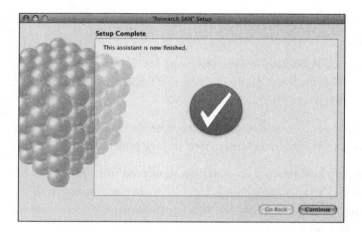

Your SAN and SAN Volume are now configured and ready for use. In the next chapter, you will learn how to manage the Xsan clients.

What You've Learned

▶ Before you can configure your Fibre Channel Switch, you must make sure that *all* SAN storage and *all* SAN clients are turned on and cabled correctly. If the equipment is not turned on and cabled correctly, you will not see the WWPN in the management window and will not be able to configure, use I/O Stream Guard, use Device Scan, or assign the equipment to specific zones.

▶ Although zoning is optional on the QLogic 5000 series Fibre Channel switches, it is required on the QLogic 9000 series.

▶ When configuring LUN RAID levels, RAID 1 is best for the metadata LUN and RAID 5 is best for the data LUNs.

▶ The recommended method of configuring the LUNs on a Promise VTrak RAID is to use the configuration scripts provided by Apple. If you decide to manually configure the LUNs with WebPAM PROe, you will also have to manually configure the controllers.

▶ When configuring the SAN clients, it is not necessary to configure the private metadata Ethernet interface. Xsan Admin will do that automatically when it configures the SAN.

▶ You should configure the standby metadata controller before the primary metadata controller. This allows you to configure the SAN immediately after the configuration of the primary metadata controller.

▶ Nine volume types are preconfigured in Xsan 2. Each of these volume types has its own performance characteristics.

References

Administration Guides

Mac OS X Server Network Services Administration for Version 10.5 Leopard, Second Edition (http://images.apple.com/server/macosx/docs/Network_Services_Admin_v10.5_2nd_Ed.pdf)

Mac OS X Server Open Directory Administration for Version 10.5 Leopard, Third Edition (http://images.apple.com/server/macosx/docs/Open_Directory_Admin_v10.5_3rd_Ed.pdf)

Mac OS X Server User Management for Version 10.5 Leopard (http://images.apple.com/server/macosx/docs/User_Management_v10.5.mnl.pdf)

VTrak E-Class/J-Class Quick Start Guide, Version 1.0, Firmware 3.29 (www.promise.com/apple/Apple_VTrak_E-J-Class_%20QSG_v1.0_final.pdf)

VTrak E-Class Product Manual, Version 2.0 (www.promise.com/apple/VTrak_E-Class_PM_v2.pdf)

Xsan 2 Setup Guide (http://images.apple.com/xsan/docs/Xsan_2_Setup_Guide.pdf)

Xsan 2 Administrator's Guide (http://images.apple.com/xsan/docs/Xsan_2_Admin_Guide.pdf)

Apple Knowledge Base Documents

"Promise VTrak: Configuring for optimal performance" (http://support.apple.com/kb/HT1200)

"Qlogic 9000 series switches: During setup, Initiators won't recognize Targets" (http://support.apple.com/kb/TA25175)

"Xsan 2: Integrating Promise VTrak RAIDs into an existing Xsan 2 deployment"
(http://support.apple.com/kb/HT1110)

"Xsan: Synchronizing clocks is important"
(http://support.apple.com/kb/TA25097)

Additional Information

"Bulletproof Zoning on Xsan"
(www.xsanity.com/article.php?story=20060312090411100&query=QLogic)

Review Questions

1. To be able to customize the block allocation setting of your volume, which volume type must you select?

2. When configuring zones on your Fibre Channel switch, how do you identify which node is on which port?

3. The default IP address for both the Promise RAID and the QLogic 5000 series switch is the same; what is that IP address?

4. How should the Operational Status and the Configuration Status be set before a configuration script can be applied to a Promise RAID?

5. Why does enabling Adaptive Writeback Cache on a Promise RAID LUN improve performance?

6. Should Initiators have I/O Stream Guard enabled or disabled?

7. What role do Volume Affinities play when configuring the Xsan volume?

Answers

1. You can select any of the volume types. When you click the Advanced button, a pane appears in which to configure the block allocation setting and other advanced settings for the Xsan volume.

2. You can identify nodes based on their WWPN.

3. 10.0.0.1.

4. The Operational Status should be OK and the Configuration Status should be Unconfigured.

5. The data is written first to the controller cache, and later to the logical drive.

6. Enabled. It should be *disabled* for targets.

7. During the configuration of an Xsan volume, volume Affinities are the names of the storage pools, also known as *asset tags*.

4

Time	This chapter takes approximately 2 hours to complete.
Goals	Add clients and serial numbers to an existing Xsan
	Move a client from one SAN to another
	Control user access to information on an Xsan volume
	Identify home directory strategies and uses in an Xsan environment
	Describe the use of quotas with Xsan
	Identify compatibility requirements when mixing Xsan and StorNext clients and metadata controllers
	Add StorNext clients to an existing Xsan deployment

Chapter **4**

Client Management

The volume has been created and mounted. For all intents and purposes, the SAN volume is functioning. Now you're prepared to make the volume *usable*. Therefore, you must fully understand how to manage clients and users based on the access requirements of your environment. For example, a post-production house that has multiple projects running concurrently would have different management needs than a post-production house with only a single project.

When you have finished this chapter, you should be able to manage clients and users to meet workflow needs.

Controlling Client Access

The first step toward controlling Xsan client access is to determine whether that client needs direct (fiber) access to the data on the Xsan volume. This is SAN-level control. If the client does not need direct access to the volume's data, the client workstation can access data through a file server or other SAN client. However, if the user does need direct access, the client workstation will need to be a SAN client.

If you have determined that a client needs access to the SAN via fiber, you can control which volume is mounted in a multivolume SAN, and whether that client has read/write access or only read access to that volume.

Adding an Xsan Client

Before a computer can use a SAN volume, you need to add the computer to the SAN as a client. You can give client workstations direct access to the SAN by following the steps in this exercise.

1   Connect the client to the SAN's Fibre Channel and Ethernet networks.

2   Install the Xsan software on the client.

3   Open Xsan Admin. In the SAN Assets list, choose Computers, and click the Add (+) button.

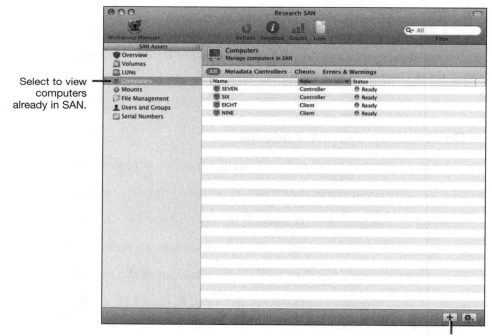

Select to view computers already in SAN.

Add button

4   In the Add Computers pane of the assistant, verify that the checkbox for the new client in the list is selected, and click Continue. If the client isn't in the list, click Add Remote Computer to add it.

5   In the Authenticate Clients pane, enter the administrator name and password for the client, and click Continue.

6   If no licenses are available, the Licenses pane appears. You can add a license in the pane.

7   In the Choose Metadata Controllers pane, verify that the checkbox next to the new client in the list is deselected, and click Continue.

8   In the Summary pane, click Continue.

Adding an Xsan Serial Number

If you have purchased additional Xsan software serial numbers for SAN client computers, you can enter those numbers using Xsan Admin.

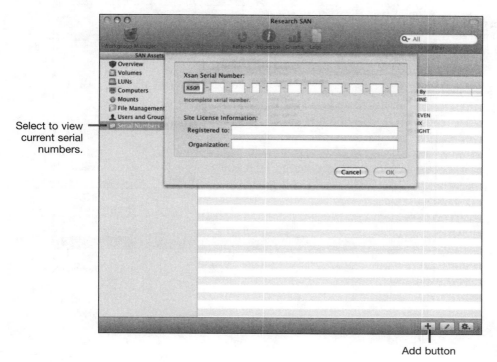

Select to view current serial numbers.

Add button

1   In Xsan Admin, in the SAN Assets list, choose Serial Numbers.

2   Click the Add (+) button.

3   In the dialog that opens, type the serial number, registered owner, and organization
    information provided by Apple, and click OK.

> **TIP** If you have serial numbers entered into a text file, you can drag the file to the
> Serial Numbers list in Xsan Admin.

Removing an Xsan Client

At some point, it may be necessary to remove a client workstation from the SAN. You can
remove a client computer from a SAN to prevent it from accessing SAN volumes.

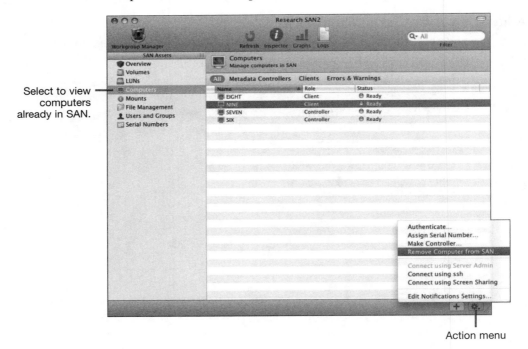

Select to view computers already in SAN.

Action menu

1   In Xsan Admin, in the SAN Assets list, select Computers. Select the client and, from the Action (gear) pop-up menu, choose "Remove computer from SAN."

If SAN volumes are mounted on the client, Xsan Admin unmounts them automatically.

2   To remove the Xsan software from the computer, insert the Xsan installation disc in the client computer and double-click Uninstall Xsan.pkg.

3   To prevent any possible connection to the SAN, physically disconnect the client computer from the SAN's Ethernet and Fibre Channel networks.

Mounting and Unmounting an Xsan Volume

Volumes are automatically mounted on SAN computers when you create them. However, if you explicitly unmount a volume from a client, you need to mount it again to restore access.

Xsan volumes are mounted on clients using Xsan Admin or in the command line using the xsanctl tool. When an Xsan volume is mounted, you can mount the volume with read-only privileges or with read/write privileges. It is most common to mount a volume on a client in read/write mode because the workstation user will probably need to write changes to the volume. When an Xsan volume is mounted on a computer in read-only mode, no user logged in to that computer can write data to the volume.

Mounting an Xsan Volume with Xsan Admin

To mount an Xsan volume on a client workstation, follow these steps:

Select the volume.

Select to view computers that don't have the volume mounted.

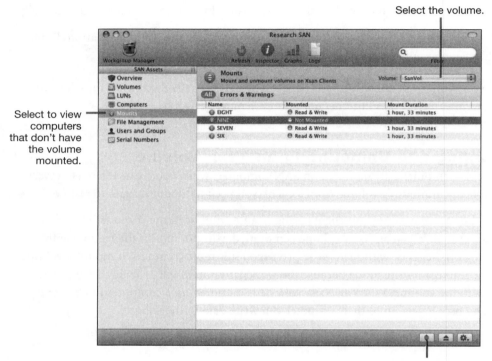

Mount Read & Write button

1 In Xsan Admin, in the SAN Assets list, choose Mounts.

2 Choose the client in the list.

3 From the Volume pop-up menu, choose the volume.

4 To allow the client to modify volume files, click the Mount Read & Write button or, from the Action (gear) pop-up menu, choose Mount Read & Write.

5 To prevent the client from modifying the volume, choose Mount Read Only from the Action (gear) pop-up menu.

A volume remains mounted until you unmount it or until the client computer user unmounts it. A volume remains mounted even if the user logs out or the client computer is restarted.

Unmounting an Xsan Volume with Xsan Admin

To deny client access to a volume, you can unmount the volume from the client. Clients can't mount SAN volumes; only an administrator can mount a SAN volume on a client.

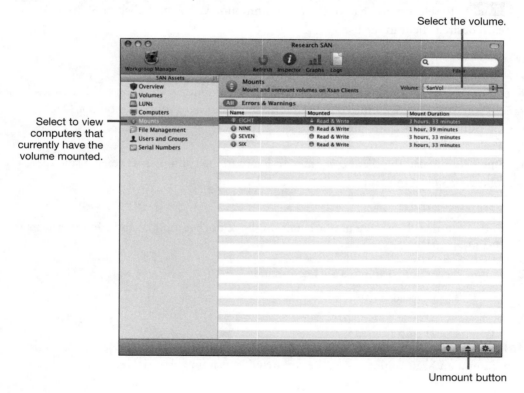

Select the volume.

Select to view computers that currently have the volume mounted.

Unmount button

NOTE ▸ A user can temporarily unmount a SAN volume from a client computer by ejecting the volume in the Finder as with any mounted volume. However, the volume is automatically remounted after a few moments. To be sure that a volume remains unmounted, use Xsan Admin to unmount it.

To unmount a volume using Xsan Admin, follow these steps:

1 In Xsan Admin, in the SAN Assets list, choose Mounts.

2 From the Volume pop-up menu, choose the volume.

3 Select the client in the list and click the Unmount button.

   TIP To select more than one client to unmount, Command-click or Shift-click each desired client in the list.

Mounting an Xsan Volume Using the Command Line

If you do not have access to Xsan Admin and need to mount a volume on a client workstation, you can do so from the command line with the xsanctl tool. To mount an Xsan volume using the command line, follow these steps:

1 Open Terminal at the client computer, or log in to the computer remotely using the following SSH command:

   ```
   $ ssh user@computer
   ```

   In this command, user is a user account on the remote computer, and computer is its IP address or DNS name.

2 Mount the volume using this SSH command:

   ```
   $ sudo xsanctl mount volume
   ```

Unmounting an Xsan Volume Using the Command Line

To unmount an Xsan volume using the command line, follow these steps:

1 Open Terminal at the client computer and log in to the computer remotely using the following SSH command:

   ```
   $ ssh user@computer
   ```

2   Unmount the volume using the following SSH command:

```
$ sudo xsanctl unmount volume
```

Moving a Client to a Different SAN

At times, you may need to move a client from one SAN to another for security or client-management reasons. You can move a client from one Xsan SAN to another SAN located on the same Ethernet subnet and Fibre Channel network. To move a client computer to a different SAN, follow these steps:

1   In Xsan Admin, in the SAN Assets list, choose Computers.

2   Select the computer in the list and, from the Action (gear) pop-up menu, choose "Remove computer from SAN."

3   In Xsan Admin, open the window for the destination SAN.

4   In the new SAN window, in the SAN Assets list, choose Computers, and click the Add (+) button.

5   Verify that the checkbox is selected next to the computer in the list, and click Continue.

6   In the Authenticate Clients pane, enter the administrator name and password for the client, and click Continue.

Controlling User Access

In the previous exercises, you explored SAN-level and volume-level control. In this section, you will examine file- and folder-level control.

To increase security and reliability, Mac OS X sets ownership of many system folders, such as a newly created Xsan volume, to the root user (literally, a user named *root*). Newly created Xsan volumes are, by default, also owned by root. Files and folders owned by root can't be changed or deleted unless you're logged in as root. But be careful. Few access restrictions are placed on the root user, and you could change system data that may cause problems.

Files and folders are, by default, owned by the users who create them. After files and folders are created, those items keep their privileges (a combination of ownership and permissions) even when they are moved, unless the privileges are explicitly changed by their owners or by an administrator. New files and folders that you create as an administrator are not accessible by client users if they are created in folders for which the users don't have privileges.

When setting up Xsan volumes, make sure that the files and folders allow the appropriate access privileges for the users who need access to them. A useful method to ensure this is by using groups and group memberships.

In Mac OS X Client, every user is a member of a default group that is created at the same time as the user account and has the same name as the user name for that user account. This user is the only member of this group. For example, if you created a user, *ravi*, on a local machine, the operating system would create a group, also called *ravi*, in which to place that user. This situation can restrict access to files and folders on a shared Xsan volume because that group does not exist on the servers managing the Xsan.

For Xsan volumes, by default, group ownership is assigned to a group called *wheel,* a system group made up of administrative users. It is common practice to change this default group ownership on an Xsan volume. Common replacements groups are called *Editors* or *Xsan Users*, and are managed centrally from a directory system, such as Open Directory, using Server Admin.

Managing Local Users

Xsan tracks file ownership based on *user IDs* and *group IDs*. In this respect, Xsan is similar to UFS, NFS, and Mac OS X Extended format. Each file and folder is marked with a numeric user ID and a numeric group ID. Ownership and group access are evaluated by comparing the UID of the file system object with the UID of the user. Permissions are applied depending on whether the user is identified as the owner, the group member, or neither.

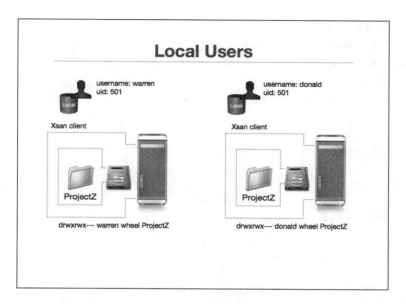

If two different users on different clients have the same user ID, files will be associated with the same user ID, and both users will have the same access. This can happen naturally when you follow the default Mac OS X installation process. The first user created by the Setup Assistant is user ID 501. All computers connected to the SAN volume will have user ID 501 if they retain the ID created during Mac OS X configuration.

This situation may work well for small sites. For example, if your Xsan clients are video production workstations, it may fit your workflow to have all users share access to the volume files. However, due to the possibility of UNIX ID duplication, users may gain access to files for which they do not specifically have permission or for which you did not intend to provide access. This situation also makes it almost impossible to meet any regulatory compliance standards through audits and the like, because you cannot adequately determine which user was using a specific machine at a given time and what he was doing on that machine.

Understanding umask

In Mac OS X and other POSIX-based systems, a value known as a *umask* is subtracted from the system's maximum permissions value (typically 777) to determine the default permission value of a newly created file. The umask can play a role in a group's working environment, such as sharing files in a group folder on a server.

Changing umask in Leopard

Default umask

	777		666	
	- 022		- 022	
	755 drwxr-xr-x		644 -rw-r--r--	

Append /etc/launchd-user.conf with "umask 002"

	777		666	
	- 002		- 002	
	775 drwxrwxr-x		664 -rw-rw-r--	

	read	write	exec
0	-	-	-
1	-	-	x
2	-	w	-
3	-	w	x
4	r	-	-
5	r	-	x
6	r	w	-
7	r	w	x

Mac OS X applies default permissions to newly created files and folders. The owner has full read/write access to local files, and everyone else has read-only access. Each operating system assigns a default permission value (such as 755 in Mac OS X v10.5) to files and folders. Default permissions exist to ensure a balance between security and access, and to see that the appropriate users have correct levels of access to a file in most situations.

Looking at the figure above, notice that there are three columns: read, write, and execute. Each row in the chart identifies a different level of permission associated with the ability to read, write, or execute specific files. A person with a umask of 000 would have a permissions value of 777 (777-000 = 777). This person would be able to read, write, and execute within the group directory. A person with a umask of 022 would be able to read and execute, but not write.

To understand how this functions, note that a umask of 022 typically results in the default permission of 755. So, assume that a Mac OS X v10.5 client with a umask value of 022 opens a file from the group folder and saves it, resulting in a permission value of 755. This happens because the Mac OS X client's umask of 022 wrote the file back to the group folder without group write permission (775 includes group write; 755 does not). Because inherited permissions were disabled on the server, the server did nothing to control the situation.

The default umask setting can be changed using the default write commands for both the Finder and the BSD subsystem to enable group read/write access by default for newly created files and folders. In the absence of a centralized directory, such as Apple's Open Directory, this can be a useful setting for enabling collaborative workflows on shared Xsan volumes.

> **NOTE** ► These settings must be made for every user on every client computer on the SAN. After changing the default umask, you must log out of the current user and log in again to enable the changes. Changing the default umask can complicate the administrative and maintenance aspects of your SAN.

For more information, consult Knowledge Base article #HT2202, "Mac OS X Server 10.5: Setting a custom umask" (http://support.apple.com/kb/HT2202).

> **TIP** ► As an alternative to changing the default umask, consider deploying a directory system such as Open Directory.

Managing Network Users

For a larger site, or if you're using Xsan as a repository for server data, your security requirements might not be best served if you give all users the same access to an Xsan volume. In these cases, the solution is a *directory service*. With a directory server on the network, each user can have a unique ID that is visible to all SAN clients. Identify all of your SAN clients as clients of the directory server, and those clients will use a unified user list in which you can eliminate duplicate user IDs.

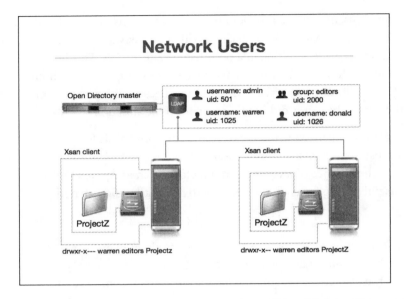

Xsan supports any directory service supported by the Open Directory client in Mac OS X. Open Directory Server in Mac OS X Server is easy to configure, but if your site already has an LDAP directory or a Microsoft Active Directory, you can also integrate with those.

If you do decide to integrate Mac OS X v10.5 clients into an Active Directory, make sure that all computers on the SAN use the same Active Directory domain and the same method of ID mapping.

Mapping Windows User and Group IDs

You can use the Windows ID Mapping setting for a volume to specify how Windows clients map user and group information to Xsan-compatible user IDs (UIDs) and group IDs (GIDs) that they need in order to access Xsan volumes.

> **NOTE ▶** To use ID mapping, Windows clients must be running StorNext 2.7. Xsan controllers and clients must be running Xsan 1.4.2 or later.

Windows clients can use one of the following methods to provide UIDs and GIDs:

- **Generate IDs from GUID**—Windows clients dynamically generate UIDs and GIDs based on Globally Unique Identifier (GUID) information in an Active Directory domain. Choose this method for Macintosh computers on the SAN that are bound (connected) to Active Directory with the binding options set to automatically generate IDs.

- **Use IDs from LDAP (RFC 2307)**—Windows clients get UID and GID values from the uidNumber and gidNumber attributes in Active Directory records. Choose this method for Macintosh computers on the SAN that are bound to Active Directory with the binding options set to map IDs to uidNumber and gidNumber.

The Active Directory binding options are set using Directory Utility in Mac OS X v10.5 or using Directory Access in Mac OS X v10.4. You can find these applications in /Applications/Utilities.

To select the Windows IP mapping method, follow these steps:

1   In Xsan Admin, in the SAN Assets list, choose Volumes, and from the Action (gear) pop-up menu, choose Edit Volume Settings.

2   From the Windows ID Mapping pop-up menu, choose a mapping method.

    If you choose "Use IDs from LDAP (RFC 2307)," you can change the ID numbers used when a directory record doesn't include a uidNumber or gidNumber attribute.

3   Click OK.

    Xsan Admin automatically unmounts the volume from all clients and controllers and stops the volume before changing the Windows ID mapping method, and then starts the volume and mounts it on each computer on which it was mounted.

If you modified the Windows IP mapping while the volume was in use, your users will be disconnected from the SAN, and users in a video production environment will experience dropped frames. It is important to let your users know in advance if you plan to make such a change.

Using POSIX and ACLs

To control file- and folder-level access to information on the SAN volume, you have two options:

▶   Use the Xsan Admin or Server Admin to set POSIX permissions.

▶   Use Xsan Admin or Mac OS X Server's Server Admin application to apply a full set of access control list restrictions.

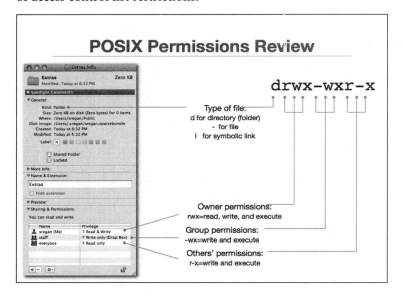

Standard Portable Operating System Interface (POSIX) permissions let you control access to files and folders based on three categories of users: Owner, Group, and Everyone. While these permissions give you adequate control over who can access a file or a folder, they lack the flexibility and granularity that many organizations require when dealing with elaborate user environments.

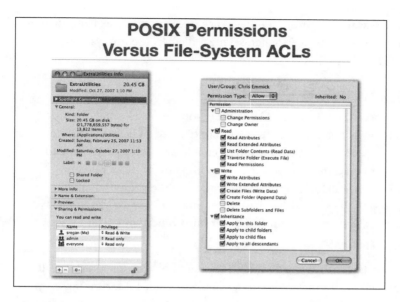

This is where ACLs (Access Control Lists) are handy. An ACL provides an extended set of permissions for a file or folder and allows you to set multiple users and groups as owners. In addition, ACLs are compatible with Windows Server 2003 and Windows XP, giving you added flexibility in a multiplatform environment. This makes it easy to set up collaborative environments featuring smooth file sharing and uninterrupted workflows, without compromising security.

An ACL comprises a list of Access Control Entries (ACEs), each specifying the permissions to be granted or denied to a group or user and how these permissions are propagated throughout a folder hierarchy. Apple's ACL model can control file and folder access using 13 permissions divided into three categories.

Understanding the ACL Use Model

The ACL use model is centered around access control at the folder level, with ACLs applied to files as the result of inheritance. *Folder-level control* defines which users have access to the contents of a folder, and *inheritance* defines how a set of permissions and rules pass from the container to the objects within it.

Without this model, administration of access control would quickly become a nightmare. You potentially would have to create and manage ACLs on thousands or millions of files.

In addition, controlling access to files through inheritance frees applications from maintaining extended attributes or explicit ACEs when saving a file because the system automatically applies inherited ACEs to files.

Implementing ACLs

To restrict user access to specific items on a SAN volume, you can use Xsan Admin or Server Admin to adjust permissions using ACLs. ACLs are enabled by default on a new Xsan volume. However, you would use Xsan Admin to enable or disable ACLs depending on your preference for management. If you decide to implement ACLs on your SAN instead of the more generic POSIX permissions, you should ensure that all of your SAN clients are bound to the same directory. For example, if you are going to have both Windows and Macintosh clients on your SAN, you must bind them both to Active Directory or Open Directory, and so on.

Refer to the following chart to confirm that you have a compatible version of Xsan running on your clients. You will notice that you will need at least Xsan 1.4.2 running on your Macintosh client to be compatible with Xsan 2.

Xsan 2 Compatibility

Controller	Client	Compatible
Xsan 2	Xsan 2 (Mac OS X v10.5)	Yes
	Xsan 1.4.2 (Mac OS X v10.4 or v10.5)	Yes
	Xsan 1.4 — 1.4.1	No
	Xsan 1.3 or earlier	No
	StorNext FX 1.4 or 2.0	Yes
	StorNext FX 1.3	No
	StorNext FS 2.8 — 3.1.2	Yes
Xsan 1.4 or earlier	Xsan 2	Yes
StorNext FS 3.1 — 3.1.2	Xsan 2	Yes
StorNext FS earlier than 3.0.2	Xsan 2	No

NOTE ▶ See http://support.apple.com/kb/HT1517/ for the most recent compatibility guide.

To assign permissions using Xsan Admin, follow these steps:

1 Ensure that ACLs are enabled on the volume.

NOTE ▶ ACLs are enabled by default, so you would have had to turn them off manually.

2 In Xsan Admin, confirm that the volume is mounted on at least one client by choosing Mounts in the SAN Assets list. Mount a volume, if necessary.

3 In the SAN Assets list, choose File Management.

4 Select a SAN volume.

5 Select the file or folder you want to protect and, from the Action (gear) pop-up menu, choose Set Permissions.

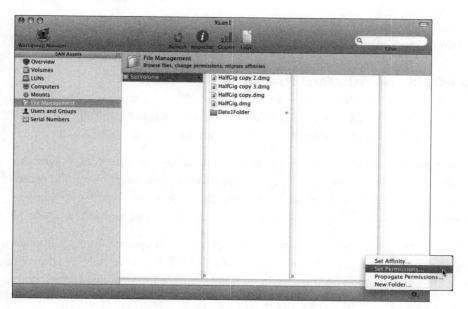

6   Click the Add (+) button to add a user or group to the ACL (Access Control List) or POSIX permissions.

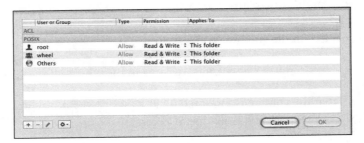

7   If you need to set the permissions for a different folder or file, select the new folder or file and choose Set Permissions, or Control-click the file or folder name in Xsan Admin.

   If you are unable to set the ACLs on the folders of the mounted volume, be sure that you have completed step 1 and that ACLs have been enabled on the volume.

You might find it more convenient to set permissions on multiple folders or files using Server Admin, available online in the Server Admin tools at www.apple.com.

Using POSIX and ACL Best Practices

Xsan Admin and Server Admin both refer to standard UNIX-style permissions, user, group, and other, as *POSIX permissions*. While access control lists technically are part of the POSIX standard, they are referred to in Server Admin and Xsan Admin as ACLs.

Permissions are searched in order from top to bottom. During that search, ACLs take precedence over POSIX permissions, but only because they are *above* user, group, and other. Mac OS X does not search all permissions for a match, but searches, from top to bottom, until a match is found. Once a match is found, the search is stopped and will not continue.

Utilizing ACLs gives administrators finer control over the ways permissions are applied to files and folders. Refer to *Apple Training Series: Mac OS X Server Essentials* (Peachpit Press, 2005) for more information on the specific options available for an access control entry.

The best practice for assigning ACLs and POSIX permissions is to avoid collisions. If you set an ACL to allow group access to a folder, make the POSIX group and related permissions the same. By doing so, you won't cause problems with applications or operating systems that don't understand access controls.

Implementing ACLs with Affinities

When implementing ACLs on a volume, you can attain an additional level of storage control by assigning affinities to the folders on which ACLs have been applied.

For example, assume you want to ensure that all newly ingested video is saved to a specific volume folder and you already have assigned ACLs so that only users in the *Ingest* group may save files to that folder. Therefore, only the users responsible for ingesting the video can write to that folder, and when those users save video to the volume, they can save *only* to that specific folder. Because that folder already had an affinity that links it to a specific affinity tag (storage pool), you can use ACLs to control some users' access to the specific affinity tag that best suited their workflow. If you did not have ACLs on that folder, you would have to trust the user to know which folder to use and to use that folder exclusively.

If you have implemented ACLs on that specific folder for specific users and groups but do not have affinities assigned to that folder, the data will be saved to storage pool(s) based on the volume's allocation strategy. You'll learn more about this in Chapter 5.

Managing Home Folders

Every Mac OS X or Mac OS X Server user account requires a home folder: a place to store user files and documents, as well as preferences, temporary items, and settings. You can use one of three basic methods to implement a home folder strategy when deploying an Xsan solution: local home folders, network home folders, and portable home folders.

Based on the type of Xsan solution you are deploying and the volume type you've implemented, your choice of a home folder solution can be straightforward. If you do not require that multiple users have access to the SAN—and the SAN clients are mainly file servers, mail servers, and so on—you may get by using local accounts. However, if you already have network home folders in place or have users that use multiple machines, you may need to use network home folders for all users. But, if you are deploying your SAN in a high-bandwidth environment with applications that require fast access to caches that are stored in the home directory of the specific user, you may want to use portable home folders.

Choosing Home Folder Locations

There are three basic locations for a home folder. The most common is the internal hard drive of a client computer, followed by a shared network volume using Apple Filing Protocol (AFP) or Server Message Block (SMB). The least common and relatively new location would be a portable home folder (PHD). Each location has its advantages and, of course, disadvantages.

One remaining location for a home folder in an Xsan deployment would be on the SAN volume itself. Although this is possible, and fully supported, the SAN volume that stores the home folder must be configured specifically for user data. In simple terms, home folders contain a large amount of small files, many only a few kilobytes in size. If your Xsan volume is designed for 2K/4K video, such a configuration would waste precious resources. It is far more desirable to create a volume specifically to support home folders.

Locating Local Accounts

As mentioned, the most common place to store user data is on an internal hard drive. Every home user and many business users—especially portable users—have local home folders. The biggest advantage to these is quick and easy access to your data. Users of CPU-intensive applications such as Final Cut Pro benefit from locally stored data because they minimize the latency of accessing files.

For a typical deployment in which the SAN volume is mounted on a computer dedicated to video editing or compositing, a local home folder and identical accounts represent a commonly used solution. When using local accounts, the administrator needs to create user accounts on each client on the SAN. This can be a time-consuming task and, worse, will almost inevitably result in inconsistencies with names, passwords, and data. Of course, it is possible to manipulate the umask settings on all SAN clients; but if you are going to do that, you might as well implement directory services.

Storing Network Accounts

Network-based accounts and home folders centralize user data and user accounts management. Home folders are automatically mounted on the computer, and data is accessed over the Ethernet network, which is accessible by a user when she logs in.

Network-based user accounts solve almost all of the issues that might make local accounts a poor choice. First, administrators can manage users in one location. User accounts are stored in a directory system, like Open Directory, and have consistent names and passwords. Each client is then bound to the directory server, allowing a user to log in from any computer on the network using the same name and password.

For I/O intensive tasks like 3-D modeling and HD video editing, network home folders on an Ethernet network can pose a problem. Data that is stored in a user's network home folder is transferred relatively slowly because Ethernet has a higher latency than a directly attached hard drive or Fibre Channel. Also, because IP protocol overhead and users access the same shared space on the Ethernet, the bandwidth available to I/O-intensive applications is reduced. Users may notice dropped frames, slow access, or artifacts in their files.

To solve both of these issues—the need for network-managed home directories and the need for the speed derived from local home directories—Apple has developed mobile accounts.

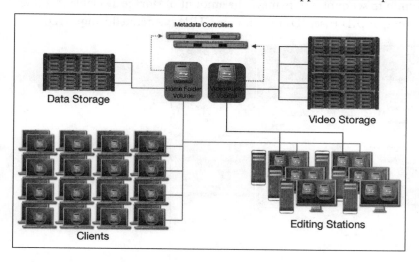

Managing Mobile Accounts

In Mac OS X v10.4, Apple introduced true mobile accounts. Mobile accounts are network-based accounts and home folders that can be synchronized with the local computer. Synchronization is controlled mostly by the administrator, but users can force syncing as necessary. The actual data stored in the home folder is synced with the server over

Ethernet to the local hard drive. This technique removes the data rate bottleneck created when user data is stored on a remote server. However, users can still log in to any computer bound to the directory server as if they were using network-based home folders. The main difference with a mobile account is that users see a synchronization progress dialog during syncing. The computer checks the data in the home folder and compares it with the home folder located on the local hard drive. Any data that has changed or is updated will be synced depending upon the rules applied to the directories in the home folder. For example, changes could be synchronized only on login and logout.

You can read more about mobile accounts and directory systems, such as Open Directory, in *Apple Training Series: Mac OS X Directory Services v10.5* (Peachpit Press).

Setting SAN User and Group Quotas

You can use Xsan Admin to set quotas to manage the amount of storage available to a user or group based on a unique UID (user ID) or a unique GUID (Generated Unique ID).

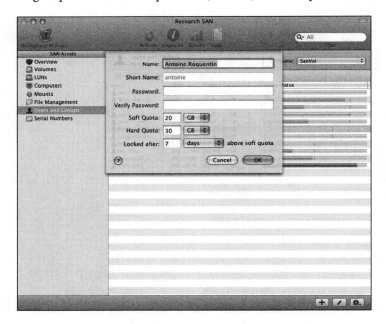

To set a storage quota for a user or group, follow these steps:

1   In Xsan Admin, in the SAN Assets list, choose Users and Groups.

    If you're not using Xsan Admin to manage users and groups, you'll see Quotas in the SAN Assets list instead of Users and Groups.

2   From the Volume pop-up menu, choose a volume.

3   Choose a user or group in the list.

    To add a user or group, click the Users button or Groups button above the list and click the Add (+) button.

4   Click the Edit button.

5   Enter a hard quota, soft quota, and grace period, and click OK.

If your Xsan computers connect to another Mac OS X Server for user and group accounts, use Workgroup Manager or Server preferences to create users and groups, as needed. If existing users and groups aren't listed when you click the Add button, open Directory Utility (located in /Applications/Utilities/) and make sure it's connected to the correct server for authentication. All computers in the SAN should use the same directory service.

Understanding Xsan Quotas

Xsan enforces two disk space quotas for each user or group you choose to restrict: a soft quota and a hard quota. You can set these in combination to establish clear limits on the amount of storage a user or group can use, while still allowing temporary access to extra space for unexpected storage needs. You specify quotas individually for each volume on a SAN. A user who has no quotas specified can use all available space on a volume. There are a few options to consider when choosing and setting quotas:

▶   **Soft quota**—The maximum space a user or group is expected to occupy on a regular basis. It is "soft" because it can be exceeded by an amount up to the hard quota for a grace period that you specify.

▶ **Hard quota**—The absolute limit on the space a user or group can occupy. Users are prevented from using more space than specified by their hard quotas.

▶ **Grace period**—A user or group can exceed the soft quota without penalty as long as each returns below the soft quota within the grace period you specify.

▶ **Soft quotas change to hard quotas**—If a user or group exceeds the soft quota for a time longer than the grace period, the soft quota is changed to a hard quota. The user or group will not be able to save additional data on the volume until the user or group members delete enough old files to bring their usage below the soft quota.

To understand how quotas work, assume you have assigned John Wolfe a soft quota of 75 GB, a hard quota of 100 GB, and a grace period of 48 hours. John's files can occupy up to 75 GB of space at any time, for as long as he needs them. If John unexpectedly needs to use additional files or unusually large files, he can still copy them to the volume, up to a total of 100 GB. Then he has 48 hours to remove the files and return below his 75 GB soft limit. If he is using more than 75 GB after 48 hours, Xsan resets his hard quota to 75 GB and he is forced to reduce his storage use. John is unable to copy or save additional files to the volume until he deletes enough to return below the 75 GB quota.

NOTE ▶ To be sure that Xsan user quota information is accurate, all user names and IDs should be consistent on all computers on the SAN.

Checking User Quota Status

You can use Xsan Admin to check file system quotas and see how much allotted storage each user and group is using.

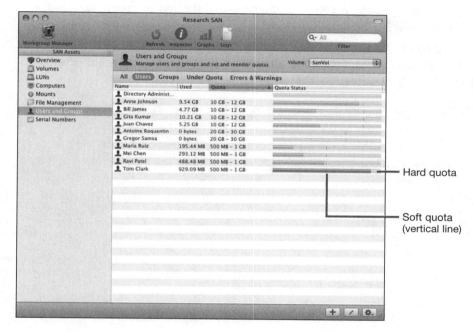

To view quota status, follow these steps:

1   In Xsan Admin, in the SAN Assets list, choose "Users and Groups" or Quotas.

You see Users and Groups only if you chose Xsan Admin to manage your users and groups. Otherwise, you see Quotas.

2   To be sure you're seeing current information, click Refresh at the top of the window.

Xsan Admin displays the following information for each user or group:

▶   Used: The amount of storage space the user's files are occupying.

▶   Quota: The soft and hard quotas. For example, "500 MB – 1 GB" indicates a soft quota of 500 MB and a hard quota of 1 GB.

▶ Quota Status: The status bar represents the full allocation, ranging from zero on the left to the hard quota on the right. The small vertical line within the bar identifies the soft quota. The colored portion of the bar shows how much space the user or group is currently using. A green bar indicates that the user or group is below the soft quota. A yellow bar indicates usage exceeding the soft quota but for a time period that remains within the grace period. A red bar indicates that the user has reached the hard quota, possibly because the soft quota was exceeded beyond the grace period and was changed to a hard quota.

TIP ▶ You can set up Xsan to notify you by email or text message when a user or group exceeds a specific percentage of the quota.

SAN client users who don't have access to Xsan Admin can use the Xsan Quotas application to check their own quotas.

Combining Xsan Controllers and StorNext Clients

StorNext is a shared file system owned by Quantum that was originally named CentraVision File System (CVFS). Xsan is fully compatible with Quantum's StorNext File System, so you can set up Xserve and RAID systems to act as SAN controllers and storage for Windows, Sun Solaris, UNIX, IBM AIX, SGI IRIX, or Linux clients running StorNext FX software.

NOTE ▶ For information about adding Macintosh clients to an existing StorNext SAN, see the StorNext documentation.

To determine if you have compatible versions of Xsan and StorNext, refer to the table "Xsan 2 Compatibility," earlier in this chapter.

Acquiring a StorNext License

A Macintosh Xsan client or controller is licensed using the single-copy serial number printed on the Xsan installation disc sleeve, or using serial numbers you purchased separately. Licenses for StorNext are purchased from Quantum when you buy the StorNext software. Xsan clients do not use or count against StorNext File System client licenses.

> **NOTE** ▶ Visit http://support.apple.com/kb/HT1517 for the most up-to-date information about compatibility between Xsan and StorNext.

Using Xsan Controllers with StorNext Clients

You can configure Quantum's StorNext software to access an Xsan SAN from a Windows, UNIX, Sun Solaris, IBM AIX, SGI IRIX, or Linux computer using these steps:

> **NOTE** ▶ When integrating a Windows client into an Xsan, you must complete steps 1 through 3 before you complete step 4, as the client will attempt to write data to the Xsan and destroy the volume.

1   Install the StorNext File System software on the non-Macintosh client following Quantum's StorNext instructions.

2   Copy the Macintosh Xsan controller's shared secret file (using the same name) to the non-Macintosh client. On SGI IRIX, Sun Solaris, IBM AIX, and Linux StorNext clients, put the file in /usr/cvfs/config/. On Windows clients, put the file in \%cvfsroot%\config\, where %cvfsroot% is the folder where you installed StorNext.

The shared secret file is named *.auth_secret*. On a Macintosh Xsan controller, it is stored in the folder /Library/Filesystems/Xsan/config.

> **NOTE** ▶ This file contains sensitive information. Secure the file for read/write access by the root user or Windows administrator only.

3   Place a StorNext license file on the Macintosh Xsan controller for each of your non-Macintosh clients. On the Xsan controller, put the file (named *license.dat*) in the folder /Library/Filesystems/Xsan/config.

4   Connect the non-Macintosh client to your SAN's Fibre Channel and Ethernet networks.

What You've Learned

▶ Three types of control can be applied on the client. The first is a SAN-level control in which the client is controlled as part of the SAN or is not physically connected via fiber. The second is volume-level control in which the client is part of the SAN but may not have mounted all of the available volumes or may have read-only access to the volume. The third level of control is file- and folder-level control. At this level, the client has the volume mounted with either read-only access or read/write access to the volume. However, user access to the data is controlled by various permission strategies.

▶ You can move a client from one SAN to another on the same Fibre Channel fabric and private metadata Ethernet subnet.

▶ Controlling user access to data on the SAN is made possible by implementing various permissions policies based on umask settings, POSIX permissions, and ACL configurations.

▶ There are three basic home directory strategies: local homes, in which each user has a home folder on her local machine and no centralized management; network homes, in which a user has a home folder on a server that is brought down to the desktop on login; and mobile home folders, in which the user and administrator have the benefit of combining centralized management with local home performance.

▶ Quotas are implemented based on UID and/or GUID. The IDs must be unique to each individual or group being managed. Hard and soft quotas can be assigned, and each user can monitor usage using the Xsan Quotas application.

▶ You can mix Xsan metadata controllers with StorNext clients on many different platforms, not only Linux and Windows.

References

Administration Guides

Mac OS X Server: Open Directory Administration for Version 10.5 Leopard, Third Edition
(http://images.apple.com/server/macosx/docs/Open_Directory_Admin_v10.5_3rd_Ed.pdf)

Mac OS X Server: User Management for Version 10.5 Leopard
(http://images.apple.com/server/macosx/docs/User_Management_v10.5.mnl.pdf)

Xsan 2 Setup Guide
(http://images.apple.com/xsan/docs/Xsan_2_Setup_Guide.pdf)

Xsan 2 Administrator's Guide
(http://images.apple.com/xsan/docs/Xsan_2_Admin_Guide.pdf)

Xsan 1.4 Reference Guide

Apple Knowledge Base Documents

"Xsan: Compatibility of SAN clients with Xsan and StorNext controllers"
(http://support.apple.com/kb/HT1517)

"Mac OS X Server 10.5: Setting a custom umask"
(http://support.apple.com/kb/HT2202)

Review Questions

1. If you purchase a number of Xsan 2 licenses and want to enter them into Xsan Admin, what is the most efficient way to do so?

2. When configuring the umask setting for a file or directory, you are concerned with read, write, and execute permissions. What is the maximum permissions value available in Mac OS X v10.5?

3. You are considering the home folder situation for your brokerage firm and have determined that you need more user management options. In addition, your management wants to ensure that all user information is secured in a central location and cannot be lost should a laptop or other storage device be stolen or misplaced. What home folder solution would you choose for your organization and why?

4. You have configured quotas on your SAN volume and set soft and hard quotas for specific groups. One of those groups has exceeded its soft quota past the grace period. What happens to the group's data stored on the SAN?

5. The vast majority of all command line tools you will see for Xsan begin with the letters *CV*. What does *CV* stand for?

Answers

1. Place the serial numbers into a text file and drag the file to the Serial Number list in Xsan Admin.

2. The maximum permissions value in Mac OS X v10.5 is 777. With a permissions level of 777 a user can read, write, and execute a file.

3. Centralized management may lead you to network home folders. However, the fact that users have laptops and may want to work away from the office provides an opportunity to use mobile accounts. Still, data cannot be lost if a piece of equipment is lost or stolen, and mobile accounts cannot ensure this because they maintain a local copy of the user's home folder. Therefore, network home folders are the only real solution.

4. After the grace period has been exceeded, the soft quota becomes a hard quota and the group will no longer be able to save additional data to the volume until its members delete enough files to bring usage below the soft quota. The stored data remains on the SAN.

5. The StorNext file system was originally named the CentraVision File System (CVFS). The *CV* stands for *CentraVision*.

5

Time   This chapter takes approximately 2 hours to complete.

Goals   List the limitations of an Xsan volume

Describe the contents, function, and relationships of the files in the /Library/Filesystems/Xsan/config folder

Identify the role of fsm and fsmpm in an Xsan volume

Manage folder affinities in relation to overall volume performance

Implement affinities in relation to controlling user access to information on SAN volumes

Increase the storage on an Xsan

Modify advanced volume settings

Safely shut down and start an Xsan

List Xsan volume changes that cause data loss

Identify the process for *destroying* an Xsan volume with Xsan Admin

Use practical and compatible backup solutions with Xsan

Chapter 5
Volume Management

In the previous two chapters, you built an Xsan, mounted an Xsan volume, and managed your clients. You may now be wondering if you should change the original volume configuration. So you may want to know more about the available options when managing an Xsan volume.

In this chapter, you will examine the limitations of Xsan volumes, and then study the /config folder and the file system processes used by Xsan. Finally, you'll finish by *destroying* the Xsan volume and exploring backup solutions.

Understanding Xsan Volume Limitations

When you consider all of the components you have to configure in an Xsan, it is amazing how easy it is to deploy a mass-storage solution to several clients. At present, you have a solution that works. It may not be the ideal solution, but it leaves you with a basic understanding of how it all went together and how you could rebuild it, if necessary. So, in retrospect, what might you have done differently? Would you give the storage pools a different name? Would you create more storage pools at the start rather than adding them later?

The following table lists limits and capacities for Xsan volumes and should help guide your decision making when considering whether to build another SAN or modify your existing SAN.

Volume Limitations

Parameter	Maximum
Number of computers on a SAN (controllers and clients)	64
Number of volumes on a SAN	16
Number of storage pools in a volume	512
Number of LUNs in a storage pool	32
Number of LUNs in a volume	512
Number of files in a volume	4,294,967,296
LUN size	Limited only by the size of the RAID array
Volume size	2 petabytes
File size	Approximately 263 bytes
Volume name length	70 characters (A–Z, a–z, 0–9, and _)
File or folder name length	251 ASCII characters
SAN name length	255 Unicode characters
Storage pool name length	255 ASCII characters
Affinity name length	8 ASCII characters
LUN name (label or disk name)	242 ASCII characters

Using the /config Directory

Xsan stores its configuration information in the following files:

File or folder in /Library/Filesystems/Xsan/config	Contents
volume.cfg	Volume settings
volume-auxdata.plist	Additional volume settings used by Xsan Admin
fsmlist	Volume autostart list
fsnameservers	Controller list
automount.plist	Xsan volumes to be mounted during startup, and their mount options
config.plist	Private Xsan Admin configuration information
notification.plist	Notification settings made with Xsan Admin
notes/	Note files whose contents were entered in Xsan Admin's Inspector window
uuid	Private Xsan Admin computer identification information
license.dat	The file in which you would place your StorNext licenses should you add StorNext clients
.auth_secret	The shared secret file used when adding StorNext clients to your SAN

Of these files, three require your special attention:

▶ <volume>.cfg—The volume configuration file provides the File System Manager (fsm) with the physical and logical layout description of an individual volume. A volume name is associated with its configuration file by the file's prefix. For example, if the volume were named BigVolume, then its configuration file would be BigVolume. cfg. Multiple volumes may be running simultaneously for each active volume. Configuration files must reside on the same system as the fsm that uses it.

▶ fsmlist—The fsmlist file tells an `fsmpm` daemon which File System Manager daemons to start. If the file doesn't exist, the `fsmpm` won't launch any fsm daemons. The list contains the name of the volume to be started and an optional host name or IP address (for systems that are multi-hosted or have multiple network interfaces). That host name or IP address is associated with the File System Service (fss) and an optional priority number from zero (0) to nine (9) that is used for failover configurations.

▶ fsnameservers—The fsnameservers file provides the `fsmpm` daemon with the IP address of the metadata controller(s). The first IP address in the list is the primary controller, and any subsequent entries are backup controllers.

All of the files described in the previous table are found on the metadata controllers. However, only six of those files are found on Xsan clients. See the following table for more information.

Xsan 2 Configuration Files

File	Metadata controller	Client
automount.plist	✔	✔
config.plist	✔	✔
fsmlist	✔	
fsnameservers	✔	✔
license.dat	✔	✔
volume.cfg	✔	
volume-auxdata.plist	✔	
notifications.plist	✔	✔
uuid	✔	✔
.auth_secret	✔	✔

File System Processes

The file system processes for Xsan 2 are managed by the fsmpm (*file system manager port mapper*) and the fsm (*file system manager*).

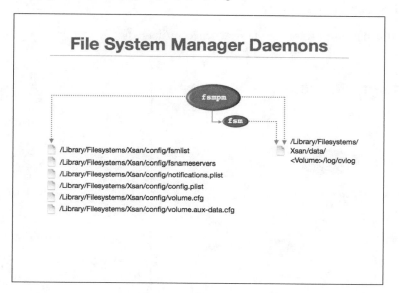

The fsmpm is a server daemon residing on each Xsan file system client and server. It registers an identifier with the system's portmap daemon that enables clients to determine the port on which fsmpm is listening. The fsmpm process publishes a well-known port on which fsm daemons can register their volume names and port access numbers. All clients then talk to their local fsmpm to discover access information for their associated service. The fsmpm daemon is started at boot time and runs in the background.

The fsmpm daemon logs information to the file, /var/log/system.log. When starting up, fsmpm reads three configuration files for information: the fsnameservers file that contains the IP addresses of all metadata controllers; the fsmlist configuration file that contains the list of volumes to start via fsm; and the role.plist file that contains the serial number, role (client or controller), and network information for the metadata network.

The fsm daemon is the server daemon that manages an Xsan volume. fsm manages the volume's namespace, allocations, and metadata coherency. It also performs I/O bandwidth and storage pool management functions.

Multiple fsm processes may coexist on one system, as long as they have unique volume names. This process runs in the background and is started at boot time. To start multiple fsm daemons (to support multiple volumes) on a single system, the fsmlist file must be created to describe which fsm daemons to start.

The fsm daemon logs information to /Library/Filesystems/Xsan/data/*volume*/log/cvlog.

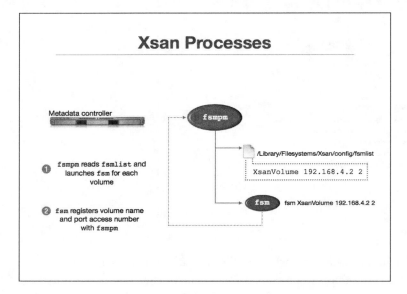

When a metadata controller starts, fsmpm also starts and reads the fsmlist configuration file. It launches one fsm daemon for each line in the fsmlist file. It also registers itself with the portmap service so that other services can find it. As each fsm daemon starts, it looks to the portmap service to find the fsmpm process, and registers its volume name and port with the fsmpm services.

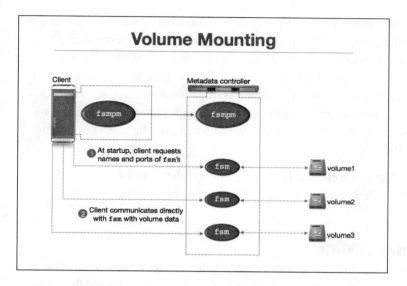

The `fsmpm` daemon facilitates discovery of volumes between clients and the metadata controller. When a client needs to discover volumes on the SAN, it requests the information from the `fsmpm` daemon. The client daemon contacts the `fsmpm` daemon on each metadata controller and discovers the name and port of each hosted volume. This information is communicated back to the client and allows volumes to be mounted on that client.

When a volume is mounted, the client talks directly to the `fsm` hosting the volume.

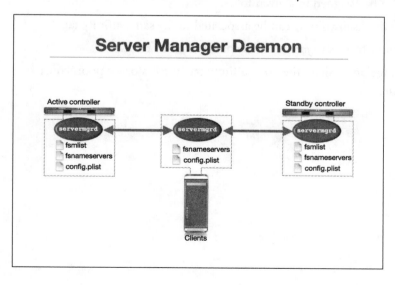

When configuring the clients, the metadata controller communicates between servermgrd running on the metadata controller, the clients, and the other metadata controllers. servermgrd is responsible for pushing out the fsmlist and fsnameservers files that allow clients to find the metadata controller. The config.plist file is written to configure the computer's role (whether client or controller), the metadata network interface, and the Xsan serial number. When you mount a volume on a client, servermgrd running on the metadata controller communicates with servermgrd running on the clients to instruct those clients to mount the volume.

Though this may seem like a process that is running only on the metadata controller, it must be running on the clients if they are to be discovered and configured.

Managing Folder Affinities

Xsan uses affinities for two distinct purposes. The first is to manage a volume's performance by directing data to the most appropriate storage pools for a given workflow. The second is to manage user access to specific storage pools using ACLs.

Before you use affinities for the above two reasons, you should understand the following points about affinities:

▶ Storage pools, or *affinity tags*, are assigned to specific folders on the Xsan volume.

▶ Only one affinity can be assigned to a given folder.

▶ Multiple folders on the Xsan volume can be associated to the same affinity tag.

▶ Affinities allow administrators to *force* data to specific storage pools.

▶ When multiple storage pools share the same affinity tag, those storage pools constitute an *affinity group*.

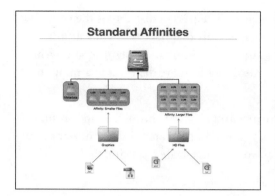

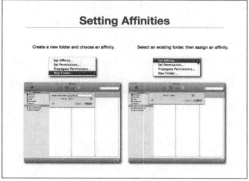

Understanding Affinities and Performance

Each storage pool is assigned an affinity tag according to the pool's performance and recoverability characteristics. You can associate a folder with an affinity tag to guarantee that Xsan stores the folder contents on a storage pool with the desired characteristics.

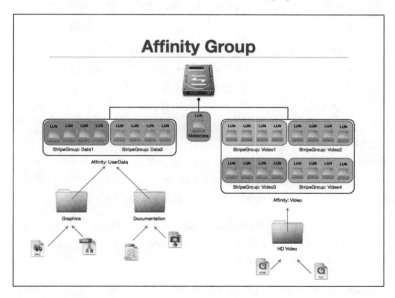

More than one storage pool may have the same affinity tag. Xsan distributes the contents of a folder with a specific affinity tag among storage pools that have that same affinity tag. This strategy improves performance when multiple users simultaneously read and write files in the same folder because the read and write operations are distributed among the storage pools and their component LUNs.

For example, if you had four storage pools (StripeGroup Video1 through StripeGroup Video4), each assigned an affinity tag of Video, you would have an affinity group made up of four storage pools. Using affinities, however, you can associate a specific folder on the SAN volume to that affinity group.

For example, you could name that affinity group *Video* and associate it with a folder called *HD Video Files*. Whenever anyone saved a file to the HD Video Files folder, she would actually save the data across all of the storage pools within the Video affinity group.

Using Affinities and Data Management

Affinities can also be used in conjunction with ACLs to implement data management strategies.

Continuing with the previous example, you could apply ACLs to the HD Video Files folder so that only the VideoUsers group could save files to that folder and only to that folder. As a result, the VideoUsers group would have no choice but to save files to the HD Video Files folder and, therefore, the storage pools within the Video affinity group on the Xsan volume.

Setting Up a Folder Affinity

Every storage pool in a volume has an affinity tag. You can use that tag to ensure that a folder's files are stored on a specific storage pool. Files and folders without affinities are stored in the next available storage pool according to the volume's allocation strategy.

Some storage pools may be configured to be larger, faster, or better protected than others. Using affinities, you can ensure that an application or task that needs speed or extra protection stores its files on the most suitable storage pool.

Using Xsan Admin, you can choose an affinity for an existing folder or create a new folder with an affinity. To assign an affinity tag to a folder, follow these steps:

1   In Xsan Admin, in the SAN Assets list, choose File Management.

2   In the columns that list the volume's contents, select the folder, and from the Action (gear) pop-up menu, choose Set Affinity.

If the folder doesn't already exist, from the Action (gear) pop-up menu, choose New Folder, type a folder name, and choose an affinity tag.

3   From the Affinity pop-up menu, choose an affinity tag.

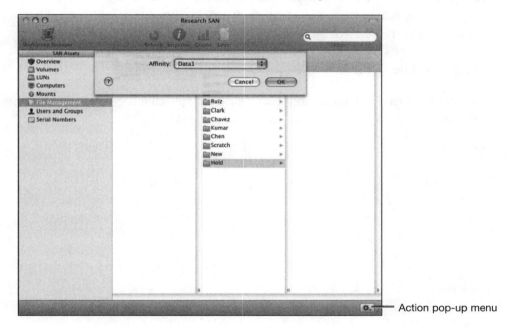

Action pop-up menu

4   Click OK.

NOTE ▶ From the command line, you can also assign an affinity to a folder using the cvmkdir command in Terminal. For more information, see the cvmkdir man page.

Removing an Affinity

You can undo a folder's affinity for a storage pool by setting None as the folder's affinity. To remove the affinity tag from a folder, follow these steps:

1   In Xsan Admin, in the SAN Assets list, choose File Management.

2   Select the folder. From the Action (gear) pop-up menu, choose Set Affinity, and from the Affinity pop-up menu, choose None.

3   Click OK.

Changing a Folder's Storage Pool Affinity

You can use Xsan Admin to change a folder's affinity so that all files newly placed in the folder are stored on a new storage pool. To change a folder affinity, follow these steps:

1   In Xsan Admin, in the SAN Assets list, choose File Management.

2   Select the folder. From the Action (gear) pop-up menu, choose Set Affinity, and from the Affinity pop-up menu, choose the new affinity tag.

3   Click OK.

> **NOTE** ▶ Files already in the folder are not automatically moved to the new storage pool. To move the files that were in the folder to a storage pool with the new affinity tag, use the snfsdefrag command in Terminal. For information and an example, see the snfsdefrag man page.

Increasing SAN Storage

To increase the available storage on your SAN, you can use three methods:

▶   Add LUNs to existing storage pools

▶   Add storage pools to existing volumes

▶   Add new volumes

Adding LUNs to a storage pool increases the size of an existing volume, and it can improve performance by increasing the number of RAID controllers and data paths between clients and storage. When adding the new LUNs, Xsan Admin stops the volume and unmounts it from clients.

Adding an entire storage pool to a volume also increases available storage and requires Xsan Admin to stop the volume and unmount it from clients.

Adding an entire volume to a SAN creates a MultiSAN environment in which you can manage multiple volumes through a single interface. Further, this allows you to balance the load and performance of the individual volumes by having them hosted on separate metadata controllers.

Preparing LUNs

Each LUN in an Xsan volume is a RAID array. The way you set up your arrays depends upon the storage device you are using.

If you're adding new RAID systems to your SAN, they may be ready to use right out of the box. Many RAID systems ship already configured as one or more RAID arrays, and each array should appear in the Xsan setup assistant as a usable LUN.

To create a different set of LUNs for your SAN, use the application that comes with your RAID system to create, for example, LUNs based on different RAID schemes or LUNs based on array stripes.

If a LUN that doesn't yet belong to a storage pool is listed in Xsan Admin with a capacity of 2 terabytes—even though you know it is larger (which can happen if you used the LUN with an earlier version of Xsan)—try relabeling the LUN.

To re-label a LUN, follow these steps:

1 In Xsan Admin, in the SAN Assets list, choose LUNs.

2 Select the LUN in the list, and from the Action (gear) pop-up menu, choose Remove LUN Label.

3 With the LUN selected, from the Action pop-up menu, choose Change LUN label, and enter a label.

4 Click Label.

   NOTE ▸ You can also change the label of a LUN using the cvlabel tool on a command line. For more information, see the cvlabel man page.

Finding a LUN's Drive Modules

To see which drive modules belong to a LUN, you can use Xsan Admin to turn on the drive activity lights on the RAID system that hosts the LUN.

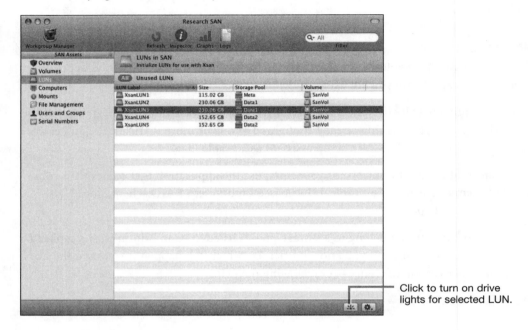

Click to turn on drive lights for selected LUN.

To find a LUN's drives, follow these steps:

1   In Xsan Admin, in the SAN Assets list, choose LUNs.

2   In the list of LUNs, select the desired LUN.

3   Click the Identify LUN Using RAID Lights button in the lower right corner of the window.

    The activity lights on the RAID system should turn on.

Adding LUNs to a Storage Pool

You can increase the size of a SAN volume by adding LUNs (RAID arrays or array slices) to storage pools in the volume. If you're expanding a volume based on a built-in volume type, you will add LUNs to affinity tags, and Xsan Admin will assign those LUNs to underlying storage pools for you. If you're expanding a custom volume, you will add LUNs directly to storage pools.

NOTE ▶ A storage pool can't contain more than 32 LUNs; the total number of LUNs in a volume can't be greater than 512; and you can't add LUNs to a storage pool that contains only journal data or metadata.

Choosing Compatible LUNs

LUNs that you add to an existing storage pool must be at least as large as the LUNs already in that pool. However, if a new LUN is larger than LUNs already in the pool, its extra capacity can't be used. For example, if you have two LUNs of different sizes and you are attempting to add another storage pool to a mail cluster volume type, the new storage pool will be twice the size of the smallest LUN. The extra storage beyond that available in the smallest LUN is not added to the total that is available in the new storage pool. So, always try to add LUNs that are identical in size or similar in performance and capacity to the LUNs already in the storage pool. Mixing LUNs of different sizes or speeds in the same storage pool wastes capacity and can degrade performance.

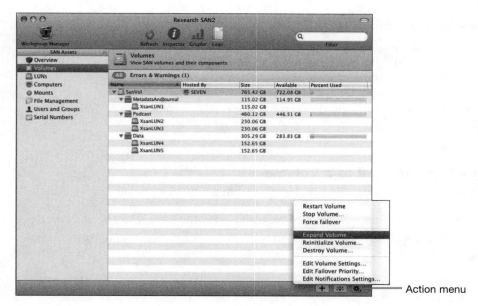

Action menu

To add a LUN to a storage pool, do the following:

1 If necessary, connect the RAID system that hosts the LUN to the SAN Fibre Channel network and turn on the device.

2 In Xsan Admin, in the SAN Assets list, choose Volumes.

3 Select the desired volume in the list and, from the Action (gear) pop-up menu, choose Expand Volume.

4 In the Label LUNs pane of the assistant, choose whether you want to label unlabeled LUNs individually or sequentially based on a label prefix.

  NOTE ▸ If you label sequentially using a label prefix, Xsan Admin adds a number to the end of the prefix to create a LUN label. For example, if you use the prefix *LUN*, your LUNs will be labeled LUN1, LUN2, and so on.

5 If you choose to label LUNs individually, click Edit LUN Label in the next pane and type a new label.

  NOTE ▸ Whichever label choice you make, LUNs that are already labeled are not changed.

6 In the Configure Volume Storage pane, drag the new LUNs to affinity tags or, if this is a custom volume, to storage pools.

7 Click Continue to unmount and stop the volume, add the new storage, and remount the expanded volume.

Adding a Storage Pool to a Volume

You can increase free space on a SAN volume by adding a storage pool to that volume.

If you're expanding a volume that is based on a built-in volume type, you actually create a new affinity tag and add LUNs to it. Xsan Admin automatically creates and organizes new storage pools within that tag.

If you're expanding a custom volume, you create new storage pools directly and add LUNs directly to them.

To add a storage pool, follow these steps:

1 If necessary, connect the RAID systems that host the storage pool's LUNs to the SAN Fibre Channel network and turn on the device.

2 In Xsan Admin, in the SAN Assets list, choose Volumes.

3 Select the volume in the list and, from the Action (gear) pop-up menu, choose Expand Volume.

4 In the Label LUNs pane of the assistant, choose whether you want to label any un-labeled LUNs individually, or sequentially based on a label prefix.

5 If you choose to label LUNs individually, click Edit LUN Label in the next pane and type a new label.

6 In the Configure Volume Storage pane, click New Affinity Tag or New Pool to add an affinity tag or storage pool.

   If the OK button is disabled when you finish typing the name, the name is reserved; try another. For list of reserved names, see "Applying Common SAN Troubleshooting Techniques" in Chapter 6.

7 Drag LUNs to the new tag or pool.

8 Click Continue to unmount and stop the volume, add the new storage, and remount the expanded volume.

Adding a Volume to a SAN

The previous sections have detailed various methods by which you can add storage to an existing volume. All of those methods involved stopping the volume and making modifi-cations. At times, you may be unable to sustain any downtime on a respective volume, or security may dictate the creation of a separate volume. On those occasions, you have two options: create another Xsan or add a volume to your existing SAN. A single Xsan SAN can provide access to multiple volumes.

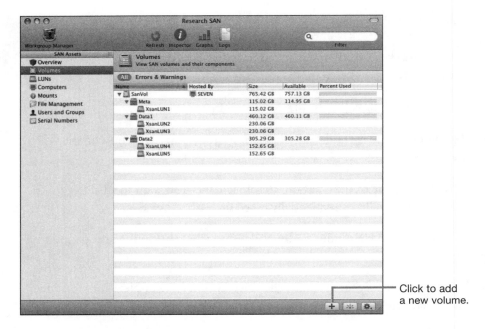

Click to add
a new volume.

To add a volume, do the following:

1   In Xsan Admin, in the SAN Assets list, choose Volumes, and click the Add Volume
    (+) button.

2   In the Volume Name and Type pane of the assistant, type a name for the volume and
    choose a volume type that matches the kind of work the volume will support.

    Xsan Admin sets the underlying volume settings accordingly.

3   In the Configure Volume Affinities pane (or the Configure Volume Storage pane if
    you chose the custom volume type), drag LUNs to affinity tags or storage pools.

4   In the Volume Failover Priority pane, drag the controller that you want to host the
    volume to the top of the list whenever possible. Arrange the other controllers in
    descending order.

    This determines the failover priority of your primary and secondary metadata con-
    trollers, with the controller on the top of the list being the primary controller.

    When you're finished, the volume is automatically mounted on all SAN clients.

5   To confirm that your expansion was successful, use Xsan Admin to check the amount of available free space on the SAN.

Changing Advanced Volume Settings

If your SAN volume has special configuration requirements, you can customize the standard settings when you create the volume. You can also change these settings for an existing volume, with the exception of the volume name and block allocation size.

> **NOTE ▶** To change a volume's name or block allocation size, you must destroy and re-create the volume.

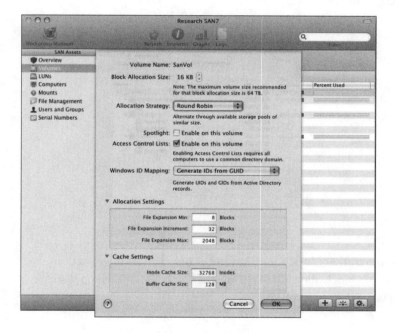

To view or change volume settings, follow these steps:

1   In the SAN Assets list, choose Volumes.

2   Select the desired volume in the list.

3 From the Action (gear) pop-up menu, choose Edit Volume Settings.

4 Click OK.

The following pages of this section contain information about each of the available settings.

Setting the Block Allocation Size

In Chapter 2, you studied block allocation size extensively when you were planning your SAN.

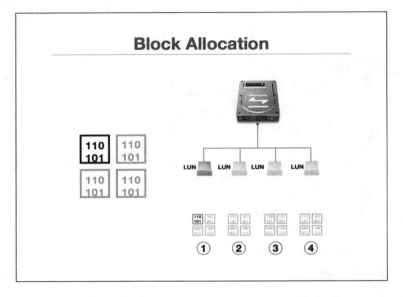

You should remember, however, that block allocation size is only half of the equation and that Xsan uses the volume block allocation size together with the storage pool stripe breadth to decide how to write data to a volume.

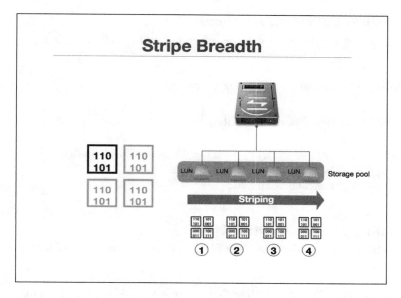

Computers running Mac OS X or Mac OS X Server have an optimal transfer size of 1 MB, or 1048576 bytes. The calculation to determine the optimal stripe breadth for your application is:

Stripe breadth = (1048576/number of LUNs)/block allocation size

For more information on the block allocation size, see "Choosing the Block Allocation Size" in Chapter 2.

Understanding Volume Allocation Strategy

You can change the allocation strategy for a volume to choose how storage for new files or additional storage for existing files is allocated on the storage pools that belong to the volume.

As you learned in Chapter 2, there are three allocation strategies:

▶ Round Robin—Each new request for space is assigned to the next available storage pool in the volume.

▶ Fill—All data is stored on the first storage pool until the pool is full; then data is stored on the next available storage pool, and so on.

▶ Balance—New data is written to the storage pool that has the most free space available.

Enabling or Disabling Spotlight on a Volume

You can use Xsan Admin to control whether a volume is indexed and searchable using Spotlight.

To enable or disable Spotlight on a volume, follow these steps:

1 In Xsan Admin, in the SAN Assets list, choose Volumes.

2 Select the volume and, from the Action (gear) pop-up menu, choose Edit Volume Settings.

3 Select or deselect the Spotlight checkbox and click OK.

Enabling and Disabling Access Control Lists

Using Xsan Admin, you can specify whether the Xsan file system uses access control lists (ACLs) on a volume.

Xsan 2 clients, Xsan 1.4 clients, and Windows StorNext clients recognize ACLs. UNIX clients ignore ACLs on Xsan volumes. If you have a mix of Windows clients and Xsan clients, they must all be bound to the same directory domain, whether provided by Open Directory configured as a primary domain controller (PDC) or by Windows Active Directory.

> **NOTE ▶** If you enable ACLs and your SAN includes clients that don't support them, don't use those clients to change file or folder ownership information, or inconsistencies might result.

To enable or disable ACLs, do the following:

1 In Xsan Admin, in the SAN Assets list, choose Volumes.

2 Select the volume and, from the Action (gear) pop-up menu, choose Edit Volume Settings.

3 Select or deselect the Access Control Lists checkbox, and click OK.

Changing Windows ID Mapping

If you have Windows clients on your SAN, you can change Windows ID mapping to determine how those clients map user and group information to the Xsan-compatible user IDs and group IDs they use when accessing the volume.

> **NOTE** ▶ To learn more about configuring these settings, see "Controlling User Access" in Chapter 4.

Changing Advanced Allocation and Cache Settings

You can use Xsan Admin to configure volume settings that allocate space for growing files and cache file-related data structures to suit your volume type. If necessary, you can use Xsan Admin to adjust these advanced allocation and caching settings for your volume.

To change advanced volume settings, follow these steps:

1 In Xsan Admin, in the SAN Assets list, choose Volumes.

2 Select the desired volume.

3 From the Action (gear) pop-up menu, choose Edit Volume Settings.

4 Choose from one of the following options:

▶ File Expansion Min: The number of storage blocks added to the file for the first expansion request.

The default value is 8 blocks, with minimum and maximum values of 1 and 32768 blocks, respectively.

▶ File Expansion Increment: The number of storage blocks by which the expansion request is increased for each subsequent request.

The default value is 32 blocks, with minimum and maximum values of 1 and 32768 blocks, respectively.

▶ File Expansion Max: The maximum expansion request that is allowed.

The default value is 2048 blocks, with minimum and maximum values of 1 and 32768 blocks, respectively.

▶   Inode Cache Size: The maximum number of inode data structures that can be cached on the volume by a metadata controller.

The default value is 32K, with minimum and maximum values of 4K and 512K, respectively.

▶   Buffer Cache Size: The amount of memory that the metadata controller can allocate for storing a volume's metadata. Increasing this value can improve the performance of many metadata operations by performing a memory cache access to directory blocks, inode information, and other metadata information. This is about 10 to 1000 times faster than I/O.

The default value is 32 MB, with minimum and maximum values of 4 MB and 512 MB, respectively.

5   Click OK.

Understanding Potential Data Loss

Although many changes can safely be made to the Xsan and Xsan volumes, a couple of changes will result in data loss. The following table lists those changes and their potential impact on your Xsan or volume.

Changes to the SAN

Change	Destructive	Disruptive
Rename a volume	✔	
Change allocation strategy		✔
Change stripe breadth	✔	
Change block size	✔	
Enable spotlight		✔
Enable access controls		✔
Change Windows ID mapping		✔

Using Safe Shutdown and Startup

When maintenance or other reasons necessitate shutting down the SAN, specific steps should be followed:

1 Unmount all volumes from SAN clients.

2 Stop all volumes.

3 Shut down all SAN clients (workstations, reshare file servers).

4 Shut down standby MDC.

5 Shut down primary MDC.

6 Shut down storage (RAIDS, tape drives).

7 Shut down servers (OD, DNS, DHCP, mail, and so on).

8 Turn off switches (Fibre Channel, Ethernet).

9 Turn off backup power (UPS).

If these steps are not followed, you run the risk of corrupting your Xsan volume because the system accessing the volume is still processing data while required components are shutting down.

Similarly, when you are ready to restart your SAN, you should follow these steps:

1 Turn on backup power (UPS).

2 Turn on switches (Fiber Channel, Ethernet).

3 Start servers (OD, DNS, DHCP, mail, and so on).

4 Start storage (RAIDs, tape drives).

5 Start primary MDC.

6 Start secondary MDC.

7 Start SAN clients (workstations, reshare file servers).

8 Start SAN volumes.

9 Mount volumes on SAN clients.

If these steps are not followed, you run the risk of some components coming online before other required components are ready. For example, you could experience a situation in which the metadata controllers are ready before your storage is ready.

Destroying a SAN Volume

On occasions when a particular volume is no longer in use or needed, or when storage needs to be reallocated, Xsan 2 has a built-in process for destroying a SAN volume. After *destroying* a volume, the LUNs associated with that volume become available for inclusion in other volumes or can be reformatted for use as direct-attached storage.

If you are going to use the storage as direct-attached storage, you will need to unlabel the LUNs and reinitialize them using Disk Utility. You could accomplish this task using either Xsan Admin or the cvlabel command tool.

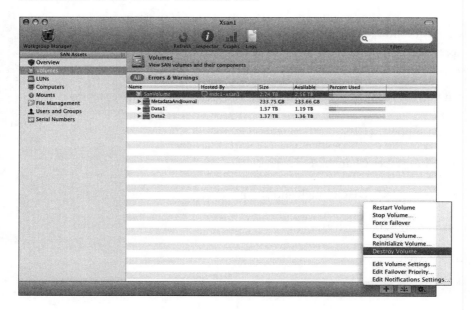

To destroy a volume, follow these steps:

1   In Xsan Admin, in the SAN Assets list, choose Volumes.

2   Select the desired volume in the list.

3   From the Action (gear) pop-up menu, choose Destroy Volume.

   A dialog appears with the warning, "This operation cannot be undone."

4   Click Destroy.

   When the process is completed, the storage pools associated with the volume are removed, and the LUNs associated with those storage pools become available for inclusion in other storage pools and volumes.

Choosing Backup Solutions

Now that you have filled this massive storage system with critical data, how are you going to prevent complete data loss in the event of hardware or software failure, a natural disaster, or some other network cataclysm? You have many options. You could build another SAN, save it all to tape, or have no backup at all. Before you can select an adequate backup solution, you should ask the following questions:

▶   How much data can be lost?

▶   How much data will be backed up?

▶   How much time is available to back up the data?

▶   For how long should the data be available?

▶   How many devices need to be backed up?

▶   Is there a requirement for offsite backup?

▶   What is the current network status?

After answering these questions, you should have a decent understanding of your backup requirements. Next, you'll need to review current storage policies to determine whether they are in sync with your backup requirements. To begin that process, it is useful to consider Information Lifecycle Management (ILM).

Information Lifecycle Management

As your information ages, it passes through a continuum of importance: from current work to archival projects that you expect never to work on again. Your storage should reflect the changing nature of your data. Information lifecycle management is a new concept that arose within the context of storage networking. The basic idea is to match your data and its changing lifecycle to an appropriate storage product.

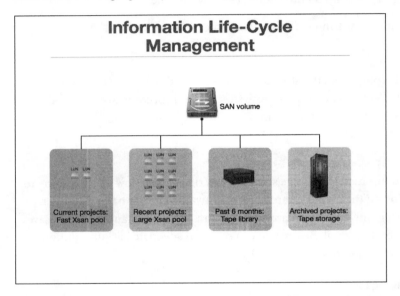

For example, your current projects may require both high performance (so that you lose no time working) and high reliability (so that you do not miss a deadline due to equipment failure). Your older projects, on the other hand, may not need the same high performance because they are not under active development and deadline pressures. Nonetheless, you may need to access them occasionally. As time goes on, those projects may not even need to be immediately available, only stored reliably. Access times of up to a day may be acceptable when bringing this archival material back online. Lifecycle management addresses these changing storage and retrieval needs.

Quantum's StorNext storage manager can help you set up policies for a lifecycle management workflow. You can define service levels for different classes of data, and automate your data placement and protection objectives. Xsan can act as a client to the StorNext

SAN volume and mount the volume. From a user's viewpoint, the volume looks and behaves like an Xsan volume.

Using Tape Virtualization

In a large-enterprise SAN, many data volumes may need backing up to a much smaller number of tape devices. This can make backup administration unduly complex.

The solution is to pool available tape resources, so that the backup application requests a logical tape and the virtual tape manager maps that data onto a physical tape. As with disk storage virtualization, tape virtualization allows multiple hosts to access storage resources without regard to the location or properties of the physical storage devices.

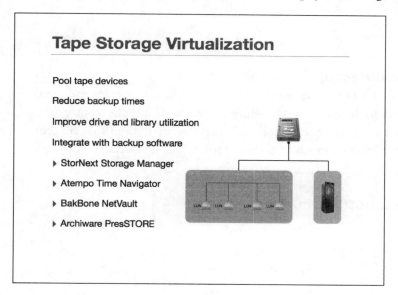

Some virtual tape managers have a large cache of disk storage—typically several tapes' worth—to minimize the effective backup time, and to manage situations in which more tapes are requested than tape devices available.

With the help of Quantum software, Xsan clients can easily access Quantum's Scalar series of tape libraries. This solution allows you to incorporate tape libraries into the SAN volume. The tape library appears as a folder affinity. Users can move files to tape simply by copying the files to this affinity. This solution requires a metadata controller running

Quantum's StorNext File System and Quantum's StorNext Storage Manager software. Macintosh clients can access the file system with Xsan client software.

Alternatively, several software packages are available for Mac OS X and Xsan that can be combined with an appropriate tape drive and provide similar ILM capabilities to your Xsan deployment. When considering a backup software solution, bear in mind that your chosen solution should be able to recognize and work with the Xsan file system (ACFS). At the time of this writing, three popular software packages are:

- ▶ Time Navigator by Atempo
- ▶ NetVault by BakBone
- ▶ BRU by Tolis Group
- ▶ PreSTORE 3 by Archiware

Applying Traditional Backup

In a traditional LAN-based backup environment, the application server reads and sends the data over the network to the media server, which writes the data to the storage device. As long as the server that executes a backup job also hosts the applications that are processing the data, SAN connectivity capabilities do not figure into the backup.

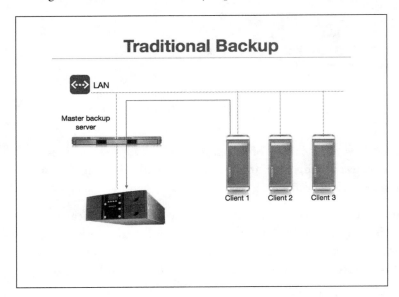

Traditional backup configurations impose negative impacts on:

▶ LAN and server performance—Sharing tape drives over the LAN is disruptive unless both the LAN and servers have a sufficiently wide backup window to perform the backup process when user activity is at a minimum.

▶ Tape library efficiency—Tape media is a cheap medium for data storage, but tape drives are expensive. A tape drive for every server is not an efficient use of enterprise resources.

▶ Data availability—Larger backup and restore windows mean more downtime.

IT organizations also spend significant operational resources on backup activities:

▶ Creating and maintaining backup and recovery plans

▶ Planning, scheduling, and managing backups

▶ Minimizing loss of availability and performance during backups

Backup functionality can be combined in one application server or moved to a specialized server and a modularized architecture. The three components of a traditional LAN-based backup environment include:

▶ A master backup server that maintains schedules and data catalogs for the entire enterprise and controls the copy of data to backup media

▶ Media servers that copy data to backup media at the direction of a master backup server

▶ Backup clients, which are computers with data to back up

Employing Disk-to-Disk Backup

Tape storage is no longer the only cost-effective backup method. Over the past few years, the cost of a disk backup solution has dropped lower than a comparable tape implementation in some cases. The cost of Promise RAID disks compares favorably to tape when the prices of enclosures and media management are factored in.

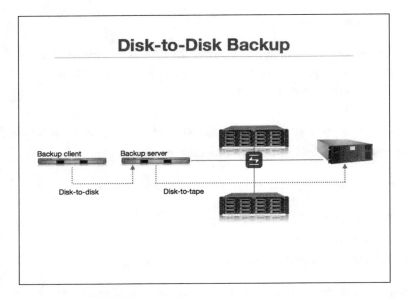

With the decreasing cost of disks, disk-based backup is feasible and offers the advantage of more rapid restore times. However, the need to retain more and more information for longer periods of time means that a pure disk solution is impractical. Most companies also need archival storage, so disk-to-disk backups are usually used in conjunction with standard disk-to-tape backups. Some vendors now offer disk-to-disk-to-tape solutions that automate the entire process.

Using LAN-Free Backup

LAN-free backup takes backup traffic off the LAN. In this backup model, the tape device is attached directly to the SAN, via either a native SAN interface or a gateway. The server takes data from disk over the SAN and sends it to tape over the SAN.

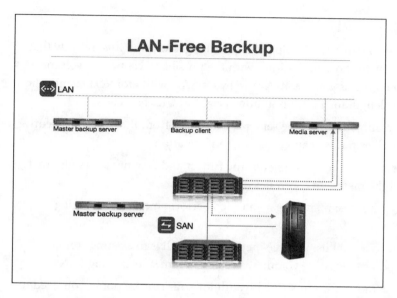

The SAN is much more efficient than the LAN at handling large data flows, which improves the efficiency of tape libraries. A smaller number of tape drives can be shared between many servers, so the cost of these high-end tape libraries can be shared over several servers and applications.

A typical LAN-free backup configuration includes a disk array, a tape server, and a tape library, all connected via a Fibre Channel network. A tape library can be connected directly to the Fibre Channel network via a bridge device.

When data is transferred at SAN speed instead of LAN (Ethernet) speed, the limiting factor for backup speed becomes the speed of the tape units. Tape units typically process data many times faster than LAN speed, resulting in an immediate gain in backup efficiency. Offloading backups from the LAN also improves the performance of the LAN for all users—another immediate benefit.

MORE INFO ► More information on backup solutions can be found at District13 Computing (www.district13computing.com).

What You've Learned

▶ The list of limitations on an Xsan 2 volume is quite long. However, it is unlikely that you will encounter any of those limitations, with the possible exception of volume size limitation. Remember, if you are integrating your SAN with StorNext clients, the maximum character length for LUN limitation is eight ASCII characters.

▶ Items listed in the /config folder on the server are different from those on the clients. Refer to the chart earlier in this chapter for more information.

▶ The servermgrd is responsible for pushing out the fsmlist and fsnameservers files that allow clients to find the metadata controller.

▶ Affinities serve two purposes: managing a volume's performance and managing user access.

▶ You can add storage to a SAN using three methods: add LUNs to existing storage pools, add storage pools to existing volumes, and add volumes to existing SANs.

▶ When calculating the most efficient stripe breadth for your storage pools, you need to know the optimal transfer size for the OS, the number of LUNs in the storage pool, and the block allocation size of the volume.

▶ When shutting down or starting up your SAN, you should follow the documented process.

▶ Once the block allocation size is set, it can only be changed by destroying the volume and starting over.

▶ Information Lifecycle Management is key to designing a robust backup solution.

References

Administration Guides

Mac OS X Server: Open Directory Administration for Version 10.5 Leopard, Third Edition
(http://images.apple.com/server/macosx/docs/Open_Directory_Admin_v10.5_3rd_Ed.pdf)

Mac OS X Server: User Management for Version 10.5 Leopard
(http://images.apple.com/server/macosx/docs/User_Management_v10.5.mnl.pdf)

Xsan 2 Setup Guide
(http://images.apple.com/xsan/docs/Xsan_2_Setup_Guide.pdf)

Xsan 2 Administrator's Guide
(http://images.apple.com/xsan/docs/Xsan_2_Admin_Guide.pdf)

Xsan 1.4 Reference Guide

URLs
"Apple Enterprise Backup Solutions"
(www.district13computing.com)

Review Questions

1. If you have an Xsan volume with the name BigVolume, what is the name of the configuration file that describes that volume?

2. Which file system process performs the I/O bandwidth management function for an Xsan volume?

3. How many affinities can be assigned to a specific folder on an Xsan volume?

4. What is an affinity group?

5. When you have finished the creation of your Xsan volume, you decide to enable ACLs. What tool would you use to enable ACLs?

6. When shutting down your SAN, what should you do first?

Answers

1. The configuration file is named BigVolume.cfg, and it contains all of the settings associated with that volume.

2. The `fsm` daemon manages the volume's namespace, allocations, and metadata coherency; I/O bandwidth; and storage pools.

3. Only one affinity can be assigned to a specific folder. However, multiple folders can have the same affinity.

4. An affinity group is a group of storage pools with the same affinity tag.

5. ACLs are enabled by default on an Xsan 2 volume. However, if you would like to turn them off, you use Xsan Admin to do so.

6. When it is time to shut down your SAN, you should first make sure the volume(s) are not mounted on any client workstations.

6

Time   This chapter takes approximately 2 hours to complete.

Goals   Add and remove metadata controllers

Change the IP address of a metadata controller

Use Xsan Admin to monitor the Xsan volume

Use available tools to monitor an Xserve, an Xserve RAID, and a Promise RAID

Identify the way Xsan metadata controllers communicate to implement failover

Repair a SAN volume using the command line

Use common SAN troubleshooting techniques

Chapter **6**

Maintenance and Troubleshooting

Now that you have a fully functioning SAN, you'll need to use the tools that will keep that SAN in good shape. No matter how carefully you planned and deployed your SAN, issues will still arise that require your attention. Some may be as simple as a user not being able to log in to his system, or an Ethernet cable being disconnected for some reason. Other issues may require a little more thought and tinkering.

In this chapter, you'll explore monitoring tools and methods to maintain and repair your Xsan volume. If all goes well, you may never need some of these tools. However, it is always best to be prepared.

Eventually, you may also discover some items you need that aren't included in this chapter. Fortunately, a number of online sources are available to assist you. Among these are the Xsan discussion board at http://discussions.apple.com and the site www.xsanity.com. For more serious issues, however, you should start by consulting the team at AppleCare.

In fact, when you decide to purchase and install an Xsan solution, which costs $100,000 or more, you should seriously consider purchasing an insurance plan to go along with your hardware and software.

Managing Metadata Controllers

Every SAN volume is managed by a metadata controller. To ensure that the volume will be available to clients even if the primary metadata controller becomes unresponsive, you can set up standby controllers, one of which will assume control of the volume if the primary controller fails.

In this section, you'll add metadata controllers, set their failover priorities, and force volume failover from the primary controller to a standby controller.

Adding a Metadata Controller

You can add one or more standby controllers to a SAN so that volumes will still be available if the primary controller fails.

Any computer set to act as a metadata controller can also function as a client. So, if you don't want to dedicate a computer to act solely as a standby controller, you can use an existing client.

1   Connect the new controller computer to the SAN's Fibre Channel and Ethernet networks, and install the Xsan software.

2   Open Xsan Admin.

3   In the SAN Assets list, choose Computers, and click the Add (+) button.

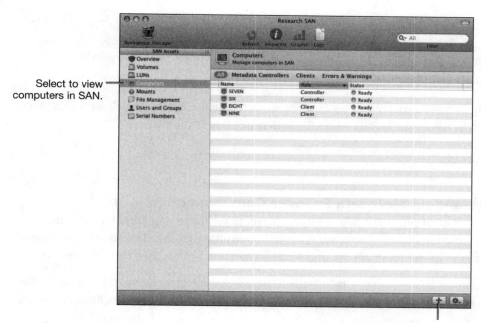

Select to view computers in SAN.

Click to add a new computer.

4   When the assistant opens, choose the new controller computer in the computer list, and click Continue.

If the computer doesn't appear in the list, click Add Remote Computer and add it.

5   In the Authenticate Clients pane, enter the administrator user name and password for the computer.

6   In the Choose Metadata Controllers pane, select the checkbox next to the computer in the list, and click Continue.

Setting Controller Failover Priority

When the primary metadata controller for a volume fails, Xsan uses the failover priorities of the available standby controllers to decide which one to switch to.

To set a metadata controller's failover priority:

1   Open Xsan Admin, choose Volumes in the SAN Assets list, and choose Edit Failover Priority from the Action (gear) pop-up menu.

2   Drag metadata controllers up or down in the list that appears. The closer a controller is to the top of the list, the more likely that it will host the volume.

3   Click OK.

Understanding Metadata Failover Communication

When a metadata controller fails, another metadata controller can take responsibility for managing the file system. The active metadata controller uses the fsmpm daemon to monitor the health of the fsm daemons, and sends a heartbeat out via the Ethernet interfaces.

If the daemons fail, or if a standby metadata controller no longer receives the heartbeat, the standby metadata controllers hold a *quorum vote* to determine which controller will assume the role of active metadata controller. When this decision is reached, the metadata controller that takes ownership runs cvfail, located in /Library/Filesystems/Xsan/bin. In Xsan, cvfail is a binary program that sends out email notifications configured in Xsan Admin.

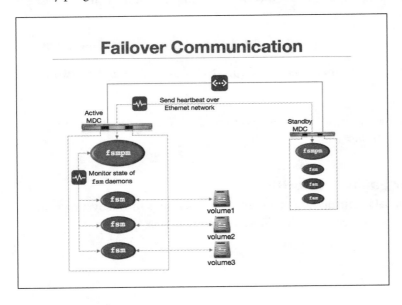

After cvfail runs, the metadata controller that has taken ownership writes to a special arbitration block on the shared metadata storage and ensures that it is currently the only metadata controller with control. The new server replays the volume journal and publishes its port address to the local fsm daemon.

If you want to take the active metadata controller down for maintenance, you can manually fail a volume via the command line. Using the cvadmin command in /Library/Filesystem/Xsan/bin, you use the select command to view which metadata controller is managing a specific volume (marked with an asterisk [*]), and fail the volume with the fail command as shown in the following figure. The quorum vote takes place, and the controller with the highest priority assumes the active controller role for the volume.

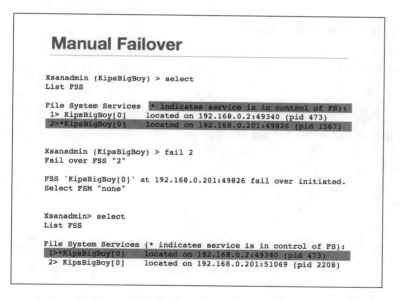

When you want to fail the volume back to the previous metadata controller, you repeat this process. Failover never automatically *fails back* without operator intervention. Failover occurs only in response to a real failure or through operator intervention.

Switching to a Standby Controller

You can use Xsan Admin to force an active metadata controller to turn over control of a volume to a standby controller. To switch a volume to a standby metadata controller, follow these steps:

1 Open Xsan Admin, and in the SAN Assets list, choose Volumes.

2 Select the desired volume in the list, and from the Action (gear) pop-up menu, choose "Force failover."

You can also switch a volume to a standby controller using the cvadmin fail command in Terminal. You will learn more about this tool later in this chapter.

Identify the Controller Hosting a Volume

Control of a volume can move from one metadata controller to another as a result of controller failover. You can use Xsan Admin to find out which controller is currently hosting a volume.

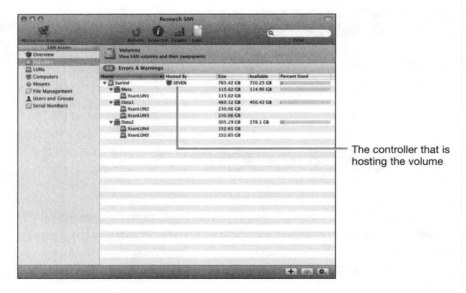

The controller that is hosting the volume

1 In the SAN Assets list, choose Volumes.

2 Locate the desired volume in the Name column.

3   Identify the host controller for that volume in the Hosted By column.

You can also identify which controller is hosting a volume by opening Terminal on the controller and typing $ `sudo cvadmin -e select`.

You will learn more about using `cvadmin` later in this chapter.

Changing a Controller's IP Address

Changing the IP address of a metadata controller can be a daunting experience. However, there are times when your IT department or other situations require this change.

Follow these instructions if you need to change the IP address of an Xsan metadata controller.

> **NOTE** ▶ To avoid losing all the data on the volumes hosted by the metadata controller, you must have a standby controller available before following these steps.

To change a metadata controller's IP address, follow these steps:

1   Verify that your standby controller is ready.

To check the status of the standby controller, open Xsan Admin, and in the SAN Assets list, choose Computers.

2   In the SAN Assets list, choose Volumes.

3   Select the desired volume in the list, and from the Action (gear) pop-up menu, choose "Force failover."

4   In the Xsan Admin Computers pane, select the controller that needs a new IP, and from the Action (gear) pop-up menu, choose "Remove Computer from SAN."

5   In the Network pane of System Preferences, change the computer's IP address.

6   Restart the computer.

With its new address assigned, you can add the computer back into the SAN as a controller.

7   In Xsan Admin, in the SAN Assets list, choose Computers, and click the Add (+) button.

8   If you want to return control of the volume from the standby controller back to the controller with its new IP address, in the Volumes pane of Xsan Admin, select the volume, and from the Action (gear) pop-up menu, choose "Force failover."

> NOTE ▸ You can also force the switch from the command line by opening Terminal and typing $ `sudo cvadmin -e "fail volume"`, where *volume* is the name of the Xsan volume.

Monitoring SAN Status

Only a properly monitored Xsan deployment will survive a catastrophic failure. IT managers and personnel who assume that a system will work forever after installation have not been in IT for very long. As the old saying goes, it's not *if*, but *when*.

Your best solution for circumventing a catastrophe is to regularly monitor the health of your SAN components. It's also important to have a mechanism in place that notifies you of an emerging problem so that a technician can address and resolve the issue before it gets out of hand. Replacing a failed hard drive within minutes of a failure will help ensure that your SAN stays up, running, and available for a long time. Ignoring problems only causes larger problems down the road.

You can use monitoring tools to track the status of the components associated with your SAN. These tools monitor the servers, the RAIDs, and even the SAN itself. In the next sections, you will examine these five tools and the monitoring functions they perform:

▸   Xsan Admin—Logs, graphs, warnings, errors, and Inspector

▸   Server Monitor—Monitor Apple Xserve hardware

▸   Server Admin—Monitor services on metadata controller(s)

▸   WebPAM PROe—Monitor Promise RAID

▸   RAID Admin—Monitor Xserve RAID

Using Xsan Admin

In this section, you'll check the status of a SAN and its volumes, and set up automatic notifications that will alert you to changes in the SAN.

Checking SAN Status

You can use Xsan Admin to view status and configuration information for the SAN and its components.

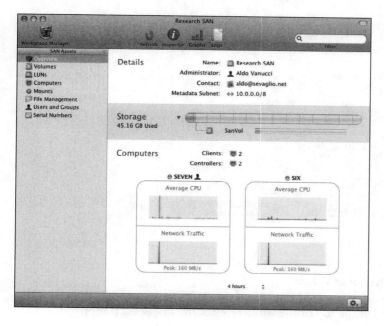

1   Open Xsan Admin.

2   At the top of the window, click the Inspector button.

3   Choose the component from the SAN Assets list or in the main pane of the Xsan Admin window.

Checking Volume Status

You can use Xsan Admin to view the status of one or more Xsan volumes.

1   Open Xsan Admin.

2   In the SAN Assets list, choose Volumes.

3   Select the volume, and at the top of the window, click the Inspector button.

Checking Free Space on a Volume

There are several methods you can use to determine how much free space is available on a SAN volume:

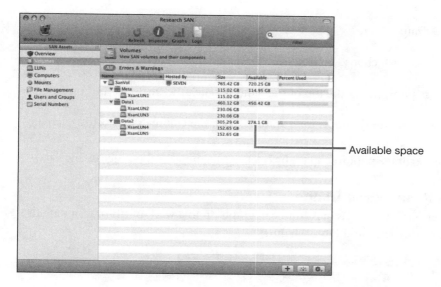

Available space

▶ On a client or controller computer that has the volume mounted, select the volume in a Finder window and look at the size information at the bottom of the window (in Column or List view), or choose File > Get Info.

▶ On a computer that doesn't have the volume mounted or on a computer that doesn't belong to the SAN, open Xsan Admin, choose the volume in the SAN Assets list, and click the Inspector button.

▶ The reported size and free space for an Xsan volume don't include space on storage pools that contain only journal data and metadata. Only space on storage pools where users can store files is counted (that is, storage pools set to be used for "Any data" or "User data only"). For example, if you create a volume consisting of four 120 GB storage pools and configure one for journal and metadata only, Xsan Admin reports the size of the volume as 360 GB, not 480 GB.

▶ You can also check volume free space using the `cvadmin stat` command in Terminal.

Checking Free Space on a Storage Pool

In addition to checking free space on a volume, you can check free space on individual storage pools in the volume.

1 Open Xsan Admin.

2 In the SAN Assets list, choose Volumes.

3 Select a storage pool, and at the top of the window, click the Inspector button.

4 If you don't see the storage pools for a volume, click the volume's disclosure triangle.

You can also check storage pool free space by opening Terminal and typing `cvadmin show`.

Graphing SAN Resource Usage

For any computer on the SAN, Xsan Admin can graph up to a week of utilization data of the CPU, memory, Ethernet, and Fibre Channel.

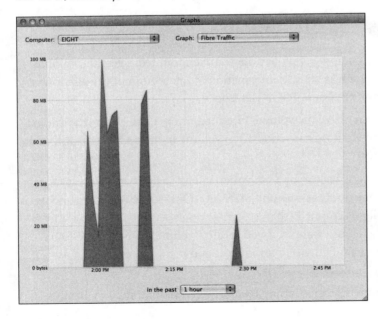

1   Open Xsan Admin.

2   At the top of the window, click the Graphs button.

3   In the three pop-up menus in the Graphs dialog, choose a computer, a data type, and a time interval.

   Memory and CPU resources used by the file system (fsm) process for a volume are listed under the name of the volume in the Graphs pop-up menu when you choose the volume's controller from the Computer pop-up menu.

You can also check the file system process's current CPU and memory utilization by opening Terminal and typing top to check the process named fsm on the volume's controller.

Setting Up Status Notifications

You can set up Xsan to send an email or dial a pager to notify you or other administrators when:

▶   A controller switches to its backup.

▶   A Fibre Channel connection fails.

▶   Free space on a volume falls below a specific percentage.

▶   A user or group exceeds the designated soft quota.

▶   A serial number is about to expire.

   NOTE ▶ To send email notifications outside the local network, the controller needs access to an SMTP server.

1   Open Xsan Admin, and in the SAN Assets list, choose Overview.

2   From the Action (gear) pop-up menu, choose Edit Notifications Settings.

3   To add a new contact, click the Add (+) button and enter an email address.

4   If the address is for an account that will forward the notification as a text message, select the checkbox in the Text Msg column.

5   Choose the conditions that cause a notification to be sent (next to "Notify if").

6 Enter a sender name.

7 In the SMTP Server field, enter the mail server address.

8 To send a test message to all recipients, click Send Test Notification.

9 Adjust settings as necessary, and then click OK.

Viewing Xsan Logs

You can use Xsan Admin to view the informational and diagnostic messages that Xsan writes to a computer's system and log.

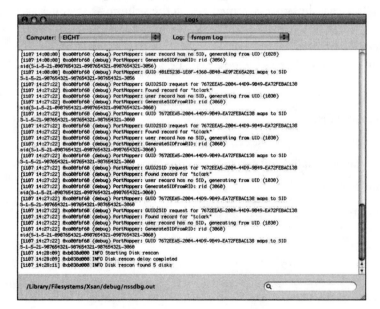

1 Open Xsan Admin.

2 At the top of the window, click the Logs button.

The Logs window appears.

3 In the Logs window, use the Computer and Log pop-up menus to choose the log you want to view.

4   To display only those entries that contain specific names, times, or other text, in the Search field in the lower right corner of the window, type the desired search parameters.

5   You can also check for Fibre Channel connection failures by choosing the computer from the Computer pop-up menu and System Log from the Log pop-up menu.

To see the log for a particular volume from the command line, look at the log file: /Library/Filesystems/Xsan/data/*volume*/log/cvlog.

Checking Volume Clients

You can use Xsan Admin to see a summary of which clients are using a volume.

To see how many clients you have mounted, follow these steps:

1   Open Xsan Admin.

2   In the SAN Assets list, choose Volumes.

3   Select the volume in the list, and at the top of the window, click the Inspector button.

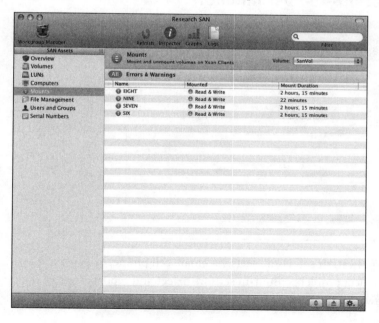

To see which clients are using a volume, follow these steps:

1   Open Xsan Admin.

2   In the SAN Assets list, choose Mounts.

3   From the Volume pop-up menu, choose the desired volume.

You can also use the cvadmin who command in Terminal to see a list of volume clients.

Using Xserve Monitoring Tools

The Xserve comes with its own specialized tools, Server Monitor and Server Admin. Each tool provides similar information.

Using Server Monitor

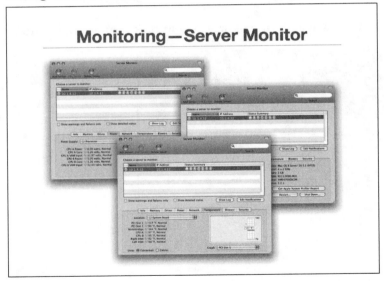

The Server Monitor application can issue alerts via email, cell phone, or pager notification as soon as it detects critical problems. Built-in sensors detect and report essential operating factors such as power, temperature, and the condition of key components.

The Server Monitor interface allows you to quickly detect problems. In the main window, Server Monitor lists each server on a separate line with temperature information and the status of each of its components, including fans, disk drives, memory modules, power supplies, and Ethernet connections.

A green status indicator signifies that a component is OK, a yellow status indicator signifies a warning, and a red status indicator signifies an error.

Server Monitor works for Xserves only. For more information about Server Monitor, while in Server Monitor, choose Help > Server Monitor Help.

Using Server Admin

Server Admin provides several ways to see a status overview, from detailed information for a single server to a simplified overview that shows many servers at once.

To see a status overview for one server, choose the server in the Server list. The following figure shows a sample Overview pane for a single server.

This overview displays basic hardware configuration, operating system versions, active services, and graphs of CPU usage, network throughput, and disk space usage.

To see a status overview of many servers at once, select a server group, smart group, All Servers group, or Available Servers group.

The following figure shows a sample Overview pane for a group of servers.

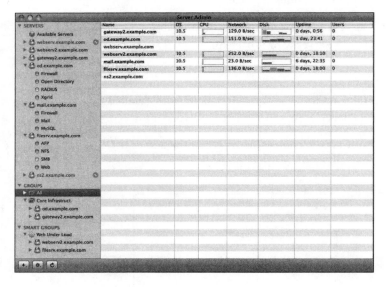

This overview pane shows the:

▶ Host name

▶ OS version

▶ Current CPU usage graph (a mouseover reveals more specific numbers)

▶ Current network throughput

▶ Disk space usage (hovering your mouse pointer over the entry displays more specific numbers)

▶ Uptime

▶ Number of connected file services users

Note that you can sort the list by column.

Setting Up Notification in Server Admin

Server Admin has an easy-to-use notification system that can inform you of your server's hard disk or software status. Server Admin will send an email to any address (local or remote) when:

▶ Free space drops below a set percentage on any system hard disk.

▶ Software Update packages are available from Apple.

To use the email functionality, the server will start the SMTP (outgoing mail) process on the server. Make sure that your firewall allows SMTP traffic from the server.

1 Open Server Admin.

2 Select a server.

3 In the toolbar, click the Settings button, and then click the Notifications tab.

4 Click the Add (+) button below the "Addresses to notify" field and add an address.

5 Repeat these steps as needed for additional email addresses, then click Save.

Using the Server Status Widget

The Server Status Dashboard widget is provided for quick access to information about a single system. It helps you to monitor Mac OS X Server v10.5 activity from any computer running Mac OS X v10.5 or Mac OS X v10.5 Server. The widget graphs processor activity, network load, and disk usage, polled hourly, daily, or weekly.

You can also monitor up to six running services and their status reports. By clicking on each service, you can open Server Admin to the appropriate service overview panel.

To configure the Server Status widget, follow these steps:

1 Add the widget to the Dashboard.

When you add the widget, you are asked to configure it.

2 Enter the server IP address or domain name.

3   Enter an administrative or monitoring login name and password.

4   Click Done.

5   To change the server address, login name, or password, click the information button
    (i) at the top of the widget and change the settings.

Using Xserve RAID Monitoring Tools

As with Server Monitor, you can configure RAID Admin to send an email or page when
a component is in trouble. For every unit, RAID Admin displays its status and each of its
components, including disk drives, Fibre Channel, and network connections.

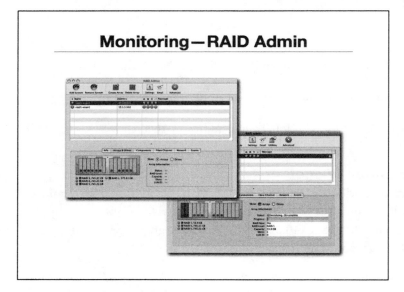

RAID Admin uses green, yellow, and red status indicators.

In addition, RAID Admin provides a status overview of the Xserve RAID units that appear
in the main window.

For more information about RAID Admin, within RAID Admin, choose Help > RAID Admin Help, or refer to "Using Xserve RAID" in Chapter 3.

To configure your Xserve RAID to send email or pages when it detects a problem, follow these steps:

1 On your client, open RAID Admin.

2 Click Add System to add your Xserve RAID to RAID Admin using the password *public*.

3 Select your RAID.

4 On the toolbar, click the Email button.

5 Enter the management password (*private*), and click OK.

6 Click the Add (+) button.

7 Enter the email address to which the unit should send email.

8 Press Return.

9 In the SMTP section of the window, enter the requested information in the Server and "From Email Address" fields.

10 Deselect the "SMTP Server requires authentication" checkbox.

11 To verify that notifications are set up correctly, click Send Test Email.

  A dialog appears.

12 Click OK.

13 Click OK to exit the notifications setup.

14 Close RAID Admin.

Using Promise RAID Monitoring Tools

The Promise RAID management and monitoring tools are much more involved than those found in Xserve RAID. In this section, you will only briefly explore the ways in which WebPAM PROe reports a problem. For more detailed information, consult the VTrak E-Class Product Manual, Version 2.

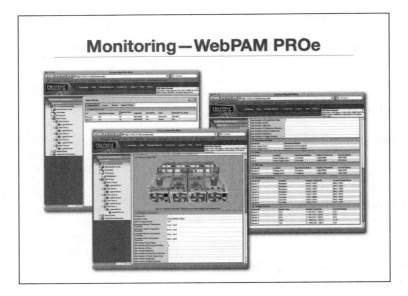

WebPAM PROe continuously monitors and reports problems with the logical drives and enclosures in the following ways:

▶ It displays yellow exclamation marks or red Xs in the Tree View.

▶ It sends email messages, per your configuration.

▶ It displays pop-up messages, per your configuration.

▶ It keeps a record in the Event Log.

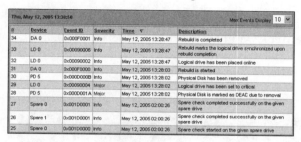

▶ It displays full information in Management View.

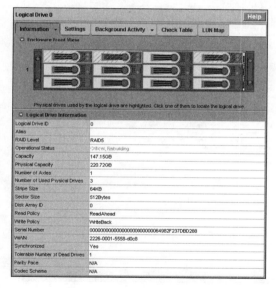

Configure Monitoring on Promise RAID

The Promise RAID allows you to report problems to multiple email addresses. These notifications can be customized for individual users. To configure Promise RAID monitoring, follow these steps:

1 Open Safari and connect to the WebPAM PROe interface (by default, 10.0.0.1).

2 In the left toolbar, click Administrative Tools.

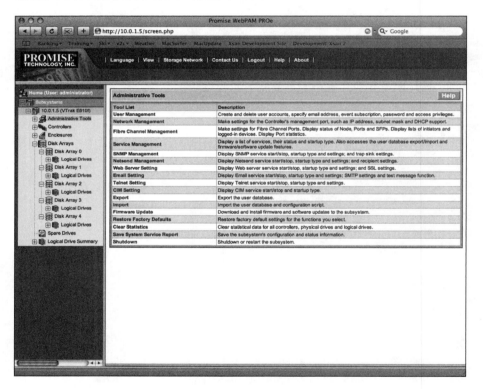

First, you need to configure the SMTP server for the Promise RAID to send the notifications. Although the SMTP server is running, it is not configured to send mail to your server and your account(s).

3   Click Email Setting to access the mail server settings.

4   Enter the requested information for the Email Server Settings.

5   Click Submit to save the settings.

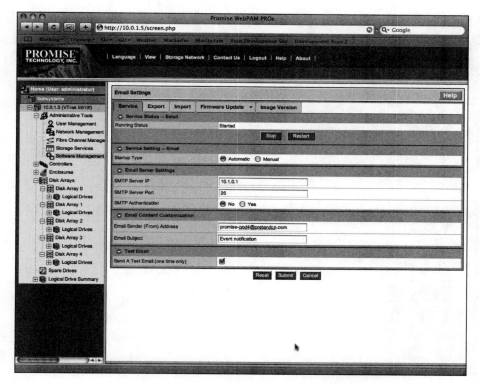

Next, you need to configure the email address for the administrator account. Because many organizations have created an email box for alerts or the help desk, you will create an additional user to receive email notifications.

First, you need to configure the Administrator account.

6   In the left toolbar, click User Management.

7   Click administrator to configure the Administrator account.

8   Change the Display Name to suit your situation.

9   Enter the correct email address.

10 Click Submit to save your changes.

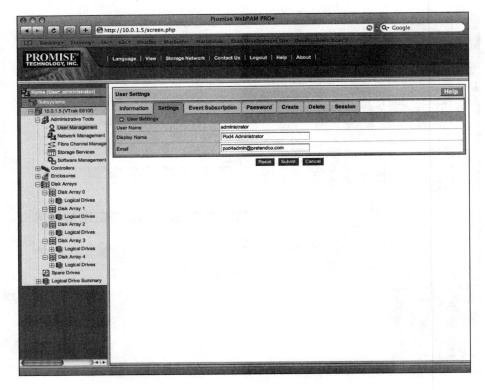

Now that you've configured an administrator account, you will create the account to which notifications will be sent.

11 In the upper toolbar, click the Create tab.

12 Enter the requested information.

13 Click Submit to save your changes.

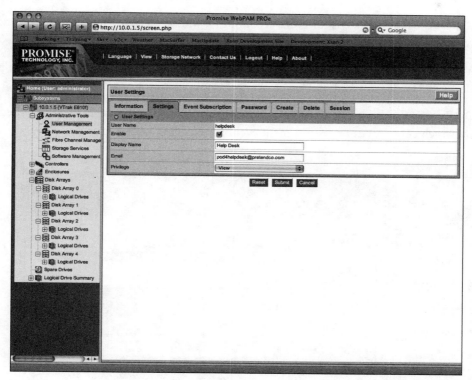

Next, you'll enable notifications and the level of Event Subscription. Using Event Subscription can be very useful in a larger organization. Some users may need to be notified only during a major outage, while you might want to notify the help desk of every event.

14 In the User Management page, click administrator.

15 Click the Event Subscription to edit the notification settings for the admin account.

16 Select the Enable Event Notifications checkbox.

17 For each of the radio buttons, choose Major (default).

18 Click Submit to save your changes.

19 Repeat the previous steps for every account that will be receiving notifications, changing the level to Info, or as appropriate, for each account.

You can set different notifications for each account. This can be useful when the help desk needs to be notified of all events and the administrator only of critical events.

20 By clicking the disclosure triangle for Event Subscription by Enclosure, you can specify which component or environment event generates a notification.

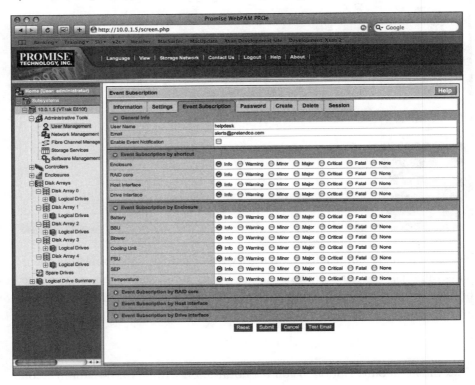

21 If you click the Help button in the upper right corner of the page, a new page will appear, showing some details about each component.

22 Close the Help window.

23 Click Submit to save your changes for the accounts you have created.

Using Popular Command Line Tools

The Xsan command line utilities are located in /Library/Filesystems/Xsan/bin/, which is part of the default shell search path.

Many commands used to manage Xsan must be executed by the root user (also known as the *superuser*). If you get an error message such as "permission denied," you probably require root user privileges to use the command.

To execute a single command with root user privileges, you can begin the command with sudo (short for *superuser do*). For example:

```
$ sudo cvfsck -n MyVolume
```

If you haven't used sudo recently, you'll be prompted to enter the password for your administrator account.

Viewing the man Pages

Even though you may be quite comfortable with command line commands, it often seems that some commands just don't work as expected. Therefore, you'll consult the man pages, detailed documentation for Xsan command line utilities. A command's man page includes information about the command, its options, its parameters, and proper use. The man pages for Xsan commands are located in /Library/Filesystems/Xsan/man/.

To view a man page, open Terminal and type:

```
$ man command
```

where *command* is the command you want to read the man page about.

Using Xsan Commands

Xsan includes the following command line tools.

Xsan Command Tools

Tool	Description
cvadmin	View or change volume and storage pool settings
cvaffinity	Manipulate affinity tags manually
cvcp	Copy files or folders
cvfsck	Check or repair a volume
cvlabel	View, label, and initialize LUNs
cvmkdir	Create a folder and assign an affinity
cvmkfile	Create and preallocate a file
cvmkfs	Initialize a volume
cvupdatefs	Apply volume setup changes
snfsdefrag	Defragment a volume
xsanctl	Mount and unmount Xsan volumes

cvadmin

The cvadmin tool is used to perform status and setup tasks related to Xsan volumes. A number of cvadmin functions can be performed in Terminal.

Usage examples:

▶ For help, see the cvadmin man page, or type:
```
$ sudo cvadmin -e help
```

▶ To enter interactive mode, type:

```
$ sudo cvadmin
```

▶ To execute commands from a file, type:

```
$ sudo cvadmin [-H host] [-F volume] -f cmdfile
```

▶ To execute a single command and return to the shell prompt:

```
$ sudo cvadmin [-H host] [-F volume] -e ["] command [cmdparam…"]
```

cvadmin Parameters

Parameter	Description
-H *host*	The metadata controller that is hosting the volume. If not provided, the local computer is assumed. *host*—The IP address or DNS name of a metadata controller other than the one you are logged in to.
-F *volume*	The volume to be the active ("selected") volume in cvadmin. *volume*—The name of an Xsan volume.
-f *cmdfile*	Read commands from the specified file. *cmdfile*—the name of a text file containing cvadmin commands.
-e *command*	Execute the specified command and return to the shell prompt. Otherwise, cvadmin continues to run in interactive mode with the prompt Xsanadmin>. If you include parameters (cmdparam) with the command, enclose the command and its parameters in a pair of quotes. Available commands are listed in the "cvadmin Commands" table.
cmdparam	Values required by the command.

Commands available for the cvadmin tool are listed in the following table.

cvadmin Commands

Command	Description
activate [volume|index]	Choose the "active" volume that you want to work with interactively. volume—The name of the volume. index—The numeric ID of the volume (to see a list of these, use the cvadmin select command without any parameters).
disks [refresh]	List LUNs.
down pool	Disallow all access to a storage pool. pool is the name of a storage pool in the currently active volume.
fail (volume|index)	Cause a volume to fail over to a standby controller. volume is the name of the volume. index is the numeric ID of the volume. To see a list of these, use the cvadmin select command without adding any parameters.
filelocks [yes|no]	Enable or disable file and record locks. Use the command without any parameter to see the current setting for locks.
multipath pool (rotate|static)	Specify how Xsan uses multiple paths to a storage pool. pool is the name of a storage pool in the currently active volume.
paths	List available LUNs.
quit	Exit from cvadmin.
quotas [yes|no]	Enable or disable quotas for the active (selected) volume. Use the command without any parameters to see the current setting for quotas.
quotas get (user|group) name	Display current quota information for a user or group. name is the name of the user or group.
quotas set (user|group) name hard soft grace	Set quotas for user or group name. name is the name of the user or group. hard is the hard quota (in bytes). soft is the soft quota (in bytes). grace is the grace period (in minutes).

`quotacheck`	Recalculate quota information for the active volume.
`repquota`	Generate the following quota report files in /Library/Filesystems/Xsan/data/*volume*: quota_report.txt—Text file. quota_report.csv—Comma-delimited file. quota_regen.in – `cvadmin` commands that will set up identical quotas on another metadata controller. You can use `cvadmin -f` to execute the commands.
`repof`	Create a report of open files on the active volume in the file /Library/Filesystems/Xsan/data/*volume*/open_file_report.txt.
`select [`*volume*`]`	Choose the "active" volume that you want to work with. The name of the currently active volume appears preceding the command prompt in interactive mode—for example: `Xsanadmin (Vol1) >` To see a list of running volumes, leave off the volume parameter. *volume*—The name of an Xsan volume.
`show [`*pool*`] [`*long*`]`	List storage pool information for the active volume. *pool*—The name of a storage pool in the currently active volume.
`start` *volume* `[on]` `[`*controller*`]`	Start a volume based on the information in its configuration file (/Library/Filesystems/Xsan/config/*volume*.cfg). *volume*—The name of an Xsan volume. *controller*—The address of the metadata controller to start the volume's `fsm` process on.
`stat`	Display information about the active volume.
`stop` *volume*	Stop a volume and its `fsm` process on all metadata controllers.
`up` *pool*	Allow access to the specified storage pool. *pool*—The name of a storage pool in the currently active volume.
`who`	Display client information for the active volume.

cvaffinity

Use the cvaffinity command to assign an affinity tag to a folder or a file, or to list the affinity tag currently assigned to a folder or a file. Assigning an affinity tag to a folder or file causes it to be stored on a storage pool that has the same affinity tag. You can see the affinity tags for available storage pools by using the show long command of the cvadmin tool.

Usage examples:

▶ To set an affinity tag for a folder or file:

$ cvaffinity -s *affinity target*

▶ To list the affinity tag currently assigned to a folder or file:

$ cvaffinity -l *target*

▶ To delete the affinity tag from a folder or file:

$ cvaffinity -d *target*

cvaffinity Parameters

Parameter	Description
affinity	The affinity tag that's assigned to the storage pools where you want the target folder or file stored.
target	The path to and name of the folder or file.

cvcp

Use the cvcp command to copy files or folders to or from an Xsan volume:

$ cvcp [*options*] *source destination*

cvcp Parameters

Parameter	Description
options	See the "cvcp Command Options" table.
source	The file or folder (directory) to be copied.
destination	Where the copy is created.

Commands available for the cvcp tool:

cvcp Commands

Command	Description
-A	Turn off preallocation.
-b buffers	Set the number of I/O buffers to use. buffers—The number of buffers to use for the copy.
-k size	Set the copy buffer size. size—The buffer size (bytes).
-l	Copy the targets of symbolic links, not the links.
-n	Do not apply command to subfolders.
-p prefix	Only copy files with names that start with the specified prefix. prefix—Characters to match with the beginning of the filename.
-s	Allocate on storage pool block boundaries.
-t	Specify the number of copy threads.
-v	Report all information about the file copied.
-x	Retain original file permissions in the copy.
-y	Retain ownership and group information in the copy. This works only if the root user is performing the copy.
-z	Retain original modification times in the copy.

For guidance on using cvcp, see the following examples:

▶ Copy the file friday to /datasets/data1/july/:

```
$ cvcp friday /datasets/data1/july
```

▶ Copy the folder /data1/ and all subfolders to /datasets/data1/, retaining all permissions and ownerships and displaying files as they are copied:

```
$ cvcp -vxy data1 /datasets/data1
```

▶ Perform a similar copy as above, but only copy files with names that begin *jul*:

```
$ cvcp -vxy -p jul data1 /datasets/data1/july
```

cvfsck

Use the cvfsck command to check or repair an Xsan volume:

```
$ sudo cvfsck [options] volume
```

In practical use, before checking whether a volume needs to be repaired, you might stop the volume and run the cvfsck -nv command. If cvfsck reports that repairs are needed, stop the volume and run the cvfsck -wv command. This command will modify the file system as needed to repair the problems and display all available information regarding the repair.

cvfsck Parameters

Parameter	Description
options	See the "cvfsck Command Options" table.
volume	The name of the volume to check or repair.

Commands available for the cvcp tool:

cvfsck Commands

Command	Description
-d	Display extra debugging information.
-e	Display file extents statistics.
-f	Report fragmentation.
-g	Print journal recovery log.
-j	Perform journal recovery.
-J	Display raw journal data.
-K	Reset journal. *Warning:* Resetting the journal might introduce metadata inconsistencies. Don't use this option unless it is absolutely necessary.
-l	Record problems in the system log.
-n	Check volume in read-only mode.
-r	Relocate files before changing volume configuration.
-v	Display all available information.
-w	Modify the file system as needed to repair problems.
-x	Report statistics in comma-separated form for use in a spreadsheet.

cvlabel

Use the cvlabel command to initialize LUNs so that they can be added to storage pools. For details, see the cvlabel man page.

Usage examples:

▶ To list available LUNs:

    $ sudo cvlabel -l [-s] [-v]

▶ To list current LUN and label information you can paste into a label file:

    $ sudo cvlabel -c

▶ To label a LUN:

    $ sudo cvlabel [-v] [-f] [labelfile]

▶ To remove the existing label from a LUN:

    $ sudo cvlabel -u lun

cvlabel Parameters

Parameter	Description
-l	List available LUNs.
-s	Display device serial numbers.
-v	Show progress display.
-c	Create a label template file.
-f	Relabel LUNs that are already labeled.
labelfile	An optional file containing information for each label. You can use the –c option to create this file, or use this file as a template: /Library/Filesystems/Xsan/examples/cvlabels.example.
lun	The LUN identified by disk name—for example, /dev/disk4.
-u	Unlabel the specified LUN.

cvmkdir

Use the cvmkdir command to create a folder (directory) and assign it an affinity tag so that its contents are stored on storage pools with the same affinity tag:

```
$ cvmkdir -k affinity folder
```

cvmkdir Parameters

Parameter	Description
-k affinity	Specify the affinity tag to be associated with the folder. affinity—The affinity tag that's assigned to the storage pools where you want the folder's contents to be stored. You can use the show long command of the cvadmin tool to see a storage pool's affinity tag. You can use -k "" to remove the folder's affinity tag.
folder	The path to and name of the folder.

cvmkfile

Use the cvmkfile command to allocate space for a file on an Xsan volume:

```
$ cvmkfile [-k affinity] [-p] [-s] [-w] [-z] size(k|m|g) filename
```

cvmkfile Parameters

Parameter	Description
-k affinity	Allocate space for the file on one of the storage pools with the specified affinity tag. affinity—The affinity tag that's assigned to the storage pools where you want the folder's contents to be stored. You can use the show long command of the cvadmin tool to see a storage pool's affinity tag.
-p	Force future extensions of the file to be aligned on block boundaries.
-s	Force the file allocation to align with block boundaries.
-w	Set file size as indicated by size.
-z	Set the contents of the file to zeros.
size(k|m|g)	A number specifying the amount of space to allocate to the file. size—A number k—kilobytes m—megabytes g—gigabytes
filename	The path to and name of the file to allocate.

Here's an example of a common cvmkfile usage to allocate 2 GB of space for the file data1 on the storage pool datasets:

```
$ cvmkfile -k datasets 2g data1
```

cvmkfs

Use the cvmkfs command to initialize an Xsan volume based on the information in the volume's configuration file (in /Library/Filesystems/Xsan/config/*volume*.cfg). Remember that initializing a volume destroys all existing data on that volume:

```
$ sudo cvmkfs [-G] [-F] [volume]
```

cvmkfs Parameters

Parameter	Description
-G	Don't display "Press return to continue" prompts.
-F	Don't display warning and verification prompts. Use this parameter with caution.
volume	The name of the volume to initialize. This name matches the name of a configuration (.cfg) file in /Library/Filesystems/Xsan/config/.

cvupdatefs

Use the cvupdatefs command to apply configuration file changes to a volume after you modify the volume's configuration files:

```
$ sudo cvupdatefs [-f] volume [configdir]
```

cvupdatefs Parameters

Parameter	Description
-f	Update without prompting for confirmation or advising of errors in the configuration file.
volume	The volume to update. If you don't specify a volume, available volumes are listed for you to choose from.
configdir	Location of the volume's configuration (.cfg) file if it is not in the default location (/Library/Filesystems/Xsan/config/).

snfsdefrag

Use the snfsdefrag command to defragment a file by reallocating its data in a single extent. This can improve read and write performance for a file by increasing disk efficiency and reducing file metadata management overhead.

Usage examples:

▶ To defragment a file or folder:
   $ snfsdefrag [-D] [-d] [-q] [-s] [-v] [-K *affinity*]
   [-k *affinity*] [-m *count*] [-r] *target*

▶ To report file extents without defragmenting:
   $ snfsdefrag -e [-K *affinity*] [-r] *target* [*target*] [...]

▶ To display an extent count without defragmenting:
   $ snfsdefrag -c [-K *affinity*] [-r] *target* [*target*] [...]

▶ To prune a file (remove allocated extents beyond the end of the file):
   $ snfsdefrag -p [-D] [-v] [-q] [-K *affinity*] [-m *count*]
   [-r] *target* [*target*] [...]

▶ To list files that are candidates for defragmentation:
   $ snfsdefrag -l [-D] [-v] [-K *affinity*] [-m *count*] [-r]
   target [*target*] [...]

snfsdefrag Parameters

Parameter	Description
-c	Display an extent count but don't defragment target.
-D	Display debugging messages.
-d	Operate on files with other than the current depth.
-e	Report extents without defragmenting.

-K *affinity*	Only operate on files with the specified storage pool affinity. *affinity*—The affinity key (in Xsan, the affinity key is the same as the name of the storage pool). You can use the `cvadmin show long` command to see a storage pool's affinity key.
-k *affinity*	Allocate new extents on the storage pool with this affinity.
-l	List files that might benefit from defragmentation.
-m *count*	Operate only on files with more than `count` extents.
-p	Prune instead of defragment.
-q	Suppress messages.
-r [*target*]	Operate recursively to defragment all files in all folders within the specified target folder.
-s	Allocate new extents on block boundaries.
-v	Display all available information and status during defragmentation.

Usage examples:

▶ Count the extents in the file *datafile*:

```
$ snfsdefrag -c datafile
```

▶ List the extents:

```
$ snfsdefrag -e datafile
```

▶ Defragment the file *datafile*:

```
$ snfsdefrag datafile
```

▶ Defragment every file in the folder /*datafolder*/ (or any folder within /*datafolder*/) that has more than one extent:

```
$ snfsdefrag -r datafolder
```

▶ Recover unused preallocated disk space assigned to every file in folder /*datafolder*/:

```
$ snfsdefrag -rp datafolder
```

xsanctl

Use the `xsanctl` command to control basic Xsan file system functions. For details, see the `xsanctl` man page:

```
$ sudo xsanctl command
```

xsanctl Commands

Command	Description
ping	Sends a "ping" message to the Xsan file system to verify that it's responding to management requests.
mount *volume*	Mount an Xsan volume on the computer. *volume*—The name of the volume.
unmount *volume*	Unmount an Xsan volume on the computer. *volume*—The name of the volume.
sanConfigChanged	Notifies the Xsan file system that it should reload the SAN configuration.
disksChanged	Notifies the Xsan file system that it should rescan disks.

As an example of using `xsanctl`, follow these steps to mount an Xsan volume:

1   Either go to the client computer and open Terminal, or use `ssh` to log in to the computer remotely by typing:

```
$ ssh user@computer
```

where `user` is a user account on the remote computer and `computer` is its IP address or DNS name.

2   Mount the volume by typing:

```
$ sudo xsanctl mount volume
```

For example:

```
$ sudo xsanctl mount SanVol
```

Follow these steps to unmount an Xsan volume:

1 Either go to the client computer and open Terminal, or use ssh to log in to the computer remotely by typing:

```
$ ssh user@computer
```

2 To unmount the volume, type:

```
$ sudo xsanctl unmount volume
```

For example:

```
$ sudo xsanctl unmount SanVol
```

Applying Common SAN Troubleshooting Techniques

In this section, you'll find solutions to common problems that you might encounter while setting up, managing, or using an Xsan SAN.

You're Unable to Connect to a Computer Using Xsan Admin

If a firewall exists between the administrator computer and the SAN computer, verify that TCP port 311 is open.

You're Unable to Install the Xsan Software

If Xsan 2 software cannot be installed on a particular computer, verify that the computer is running Mac OS X v10.5 or Mac OS X Server v10.5.

Some Computers Aren't Listed in Xsan Admin

If you want to add a computer to the SAN as a metadata controller or client and it is not listed in Xsan Admin, verify that:

▶ You have installed the Xsan software on the computer.

▶ The computer is powered on.

▶ The computer is not sleeping and is not set to sleep (in the Energy Saver pane of System Preferences).

▶ The computer is on the same TCP/IP subnets as the other SAN components. (If you are using both a private and a public Ethernet network, all SAN components must be connected to both.)

You're Unable to Mount a Volume on a Client

▶ Try restarting the client computer, and then try again.

▶ Check that all Fibre Channel cables are plugged in.

▶ Verify that no other volumes are mounted on the client with the same name as the Xsan volume.

RAID LUNs Aren't Accessible over Fibre Channel

▶ Try restarting the computer that doesn't see the LUNs.

▶ Check the configuration of the Fibre Channel switch to ensure that the SAN components are in the same Fibre Channel zone.

Files and Folders Created by Mac OS 9 Computers Show the Wrong Creation Date

A computer running Mac OS 9 can store files or folders on an Xsan volume that is shared using the AFP service of Mac OS X Server. However, the creation date for those items as reported by the Finder's Get Info command on the Mac OS 9 computer will always be Feb 4, 2040. A computer running Max OS X reports a blank creation date for the same files and folders. In both cases, the correct creation date is displayed in the Modified field.

You Have Problems Using Command Line Tools

If you get the error response "Cannot list FSS - reason - Bad file descriptor" when you run the cvadmin tool, verify that you have root user privileges. Log in as the root user or use the sudo command ($ sudo cvadmin) to run the tool.

A LUN Doesn't Have as Much Space as Expected

To enable striping across LUNs, Xsan automatically adjusts LUN sizes to make all LUNs on a storage pool the same size as the smallest LUN on the pool. Xsan doesn't access the extra space on larger LUNs when you mix LUNs of different sizes on a single storage pool.

You're Unable to Rename an Xsan Volume in the Finder

Xsan doesn't allow a mounted Xsan volume to be renamed using the Finder. To rename an Xsan volume, reinitialize the volume using Xsan Admin.

You're Unable to Add a Storage Pool

Some names are reserved names and cannot be used to name a storage pool (see the following table). If you enter one of these names, the OK button in the storage pool sheet is disabled.

Reserved Storage Pool Names

Affinity	InodeExpandInc	Rtios
AllocationStrategy	InodeExpandMax	RtiosReserve
AttrTokenSize	InodeExpandMin	Rtmb
BrIs	IoHangLimitSecs	RtmbReserve
BrlTime	Journal	RtTokenTimeout
BufferCacheSize	JournalIcBufNum	Sectors
BufferPoolSize	JournalIcBufSize	SectorSize
BWMFields	JournalSize	Static
DataMigration	Log	StaticInodes
DataMigrationThreadPoolSize	MaxConnections	Status
Debug	MaxLogs	Sticky
DeviceName	MaxLogSize	StripeBreadth
DirCacheSize	MaxMBPerClientReserve	StripeClusters
DirFDCacheSize	Mbufs	StripeGroup
DirWarp	MbufSize	ThreadPoolSize
Disabled	MetaData	Type
Disk	MirrorGroup	UnixFabricationOnWindows
DiskType	MirrorReadMethod	UnixNobodyUidOnWindows
Enabled	MultiPathMethod	UnixNobodyGidOnWindows
Exclusive	No	UnixFileCreationMode
ForcePerfectFit	Node	UnixDirectoryCreation
ForceStripeAlignment	OpHangLimitSecs	WindowSecurity
FSBlockSize	Quotas	Write
GlobalSuperUser	Read	Yes
InodeCacheSize	Regular	
InodeDeleteMax	Rotate	

Fibre Channel Performance Is Poorer Than Expected

Mismatched optical transceivers (GBICs) can cause Fibre Channel communication errors and degrade SAN performance. To ensure good performance, use identical transceivers (same manufacturer and model number) on both ends of your Fibre Channel cables.

A Client Is Unable to Use a Volume After a Fibre Channel Interruption

If a client loses its Fibre Channel connection to the SAN (because a cable is unplugged, for example), the client might not recognize LUNs in an Xsan volume when the connection is restored. If this happens, restart the client to remount the volume.

If a problem persists, restart all SAN devices. Restart RAID systems first; then continue with SAN controllers; and finally, restart all clients.

Check Whether a Computer Is Seeing Xsan Volume LUNs

Open Disk Utility on the computer and look for the LUNs in the list of disks and volumes. You can also check for accessible LUNs in Terminal by using the `cvlabel -l` command or the `diskutil list` commands.

You're Unable to Add LUNs to a Storage Pool

You can't add a new LUN to an existing storage pool unless the LUN is at least as large as the common LUN size for the pool. (The common LUN size is the size of the smallest LUN you added when you created the pool.) You can add a larger LUN, but space beyond the common LUN size isn't used.

You can only expand storage pools that can be used for user data. You can't add a LUN to an existing storage pool if the storage pool can be used only for journaling and metadata. If you want to add journaling and metadata storage, add another storage pool to be used for journaling and metadata.

Check the Common LUN Size for a Storage Pool

In Xsan Admin, in the SAN Assets list, choose Volumes, and then click the disclosure triangles in the list of volumes to show the LUNs in the storage pool of interest. Compare the listed LUN sizes.

Check the Size of the LUN You Want to Add

In Xsan Admin, in the SAN Assets list, choose LUNs, and then click Unused LUNs. Check the listed size for the LUN of interest.

Check the Data Types on a Storage Pool

In Xsan Admin, in the SAN Assets list, choose Volumes, and then click the disclosure triangles in the list of volumes to show the storage pool of interest. Double-click the storage pool in the list, and in the Inspector window, look next to Used For. This will show you the data types on the selected storage pool.

The Capacity of a Larger LUN Is Listed as 2 Terabytes

If a LUN that doesn't yet belong to a storage pool is listed in Xsan Admin with a capacity of 2 TB, even though you know it is larger (which can happen if you used the LUN with an earlier version of Xsan), try relabeling the LUN.

In Xsan Admin, in the SAN Assets list, choose LUNs. Select the desired LUN in the list, and choose Remove LUN Label from the Action (gear) pop-up menu. With the LUN still selected, choose Change LUN label from the Action pop-up menu, and enter a new label.

File Copying Doesn't Finish

If the Ethernet connection to a metadata controller is lost, Finder file-copy operations in progress on clients may not finish, even though the volume successfully fails over to a standby controller. To allow the copy operation to finish, reconnect the disconnected controller to the SAN's Ethernet network.

What You've Learned

▶ You can add or remove metadata controllers from an existing Xsan as long as you follow the steps outlined in this chapter. If you remove a primary metadata controller without first failing the volume(s) to a secondary metadata controller, you risk data loss.

▶ Although you should avoid changing the IP address of a server, especially a metadata controller, you can do so safely if the appropriate method is followed.

▶ Several tools are available to monitor the state of your SAN. Depending on the components you wish to monitor, you might use RAID Admin, Server Admin, Server Monitor, Xsan Admin, or WebPAM PROe.

▶ When a metadata controller fails, the controller that takes over runs cvfail, which sends out an email notification configured in Xsan Admin.

▶ In most cases you can repair a SAN volume using the cvfsck command. If this does not work, you should contact AppleCare.

▶ When your SAN volume fails to mount on a machine on which it was previously mounted, you should check the /Volumes directory to ensure that an instance of that volume is not already present.

References

Administration Guides

Mac OS X Server Administration v10.5 Second Edition
(http://images.apple.com/server/macosx/docs/Server_Administration_v10.5_2nd_Ed.pdf)

Mac OS X Server: User Management for Version 10.5 Leopard
(http://images.apple.com/server/macosx/docs/User_Management_v10.5.mnl.pdf)

VTrak E-Class/J-Class Quick Start Guide, Version 1.0, Firmware 3.29
(www.promise.com/apple/Apple_VTrak_E-J-Class_%20QSG_v1.0_final.pdf)

VTrak E-Class Product Manual, Version 2.0
(www.promise.com/apple/VTrak_E-Class_PM_v2.pdf)

Xsan 2 Setup Guide
(http://images.apple.com/xsan/docs/Xsan_2_Setup_Guide.pdf)

Xsan 2 Administrator's Guide
(http://images.apple.com/xsan/docs/Xsan_2_Admin_Guide.pdf)

Xsan 1.4 Reference Guide

Apple Knowledge Base Documents
"Promise VTrak: Configuring for optimal performance"
(http://support.apple.com/kb/HT1200)

Review Questions

1. Using Xsan Admin, you can identify the controller currently hosting a volume. How would you do so using SSH?

2. Although you can configure Xsan Admin to send notifications regarding the SAN volume, what other components are also monitored?

3. When using WebPAM PROe to configure management and notifications on a Promise RAID, what must you configure before the RAID can send those notifications?

4. A number of command line tools are available with Xsan. Where would you find more information about those tools and their options?

5. While troubleshooting, you discover that a client does not mount the SAN volume, and you need to determine whether the client can see any of the RAID LUNs. What tool would you use to accomplish this?

Answers

1. Depending on the installation, you will probably SSH into the metadata controller with the ssh root@*serveraddress*. You would SSH as root, as most of the troubleshooting commands have to be run from root anyway. After you were connected remotely to the server, you would run the cvadmin -e select command. When you do not have access to Xsan Admin and have to connect remotely into a SAN, SSH is the tool to use.

2. Xsan Admin also monitors Fibre Channel connections, and quota information.

3. Although SMTP is running on the Promise RAID by default, it is not configured. You must do this before your RAID can send notifications.

4. The best information source for Xsan command line tools is the man pages. The man pages for Xsan commands are located in /Library/Filesystems/Xsan/man/.

5. The easiest way to determine whether a client can see the SAN storage is to open Disk Utility.

Index

The Apple Pro Training Series

The official curriculum of the Apple Pro Training and Certification Program, the Apple Pro Training books are comprehensive, self-paced courses written by acknowledged experts in the field. Focused lessons take you step by-step through the process of creating real-world digital video or audio projects, while lesson files on the companion DVD and ample illustrations help you master techniques fast. In addition, lesson goals and time estimates help you plan your time, while chapter review questions summarize what you've learned.

Final Cut Pro 6
0-321-50265-5

Cut a scene from the USA Network television series *Monk*, create a promo for Seaworld's *Belief* documentary, master filters and effects as you edit a segment of BBC's *Living Color*. In this best-selling guide, Diana Weynand starts with basic video editing techniques and takes you all the way through Final Cut Pro's powerful advanced features. You'll learn to mark and edit clips, mix sound, add titles, create transitions, apply filters, and more.

Final Cut Pro 6: Beyond the Basics
0-321-50912-9

Director and editor Michael Wohl shows how to master advanced trimming techniques, make polished transitions, work with nested sequences, edit multi-camera projects, create fantastic effects, color-correct your video, and composite like a pro. Also covers Soundtrack Pro, and managing clips and media.

The Craft of Editing with Final Cut Pro
0-321-52036-X

Superbly fitted to a semester-length course, this is the ideal curriculum for a hands-on exploration of advanced editing. Director and editor Michael Wohl shares must-know techniques for cutting dialogue scenes, action scenes, fight and chase scenes, documentaries, comedy, music videos, multi-camera projects, and more. Two DVD-9s of professional footage and project files give students the chance to work with every genre as they learn.

Motion Graphics and Effects in Final Cut Studio 2
0-321-50940-4

This practical approach focuses on just the parts of Final Cut Studio that editors and designers need to create motion graphics in their daily work.

Motion 3
0-321-50910-2

Top commercial artists show you how to harness Motion's behavior-based animations, particles, filters, effects, tracking, and 3D capabilities.

Soundtrack Pro 2
0-321-50266-3

Audio producer Martin Sitter is your guide to the only professional audio post application designed specifically for the Final Cut editor.

DVD Studio Pro 4, Second Edition
0-321-50189-6

Learn to author professional DVDs with this best-selling guide. Build three complete DVDs, including the DVD for the Oscar-nominated *Born into Brothels* documentary.

Color
0-321-50911-0

This guide to Apple's masterful new color grading software starts with the basics of color correction and moves on to the fine points of secondary grading, tracking, and advanced effects.

Apple Pro Training Series: Logic Pro 8 and Logic Express 8
0-321-50292-2

Create, mix, and polish your musical creations using Apple's pro audio software.

Apple Pro Training Series: Logic Pro 8 Beyond the Basics
0-321-50288-4

Comprehensive guide takes you through Logic's powerful advanced features.

Apple Pro Training Series: Shake 4
0-321-25609-3

Apple-certified guide uses stunning real world sequences to reveal the wizardry of Shake 4.

Encyclopedia of Visual Effects
0-321-30334-2

Ultimate recipe book for visual effects artists working in Shake, Motion and Adobe After Effects.

Encyclopedia of Color Correction
0-321-43231-2

Comprehensive training in the real-world color correction and management skills editing pros use every day in the field.

Aperture 1.5
0-321-49662-0

The best way to learn Aperture's powerful photo-editing, image-retouching, proofing, publishing, and archiving features.

Final Cut Express 4
0-321-53467-0

The only Apple-authorized guide to Final Cut Express 4 has you making movie magic in no time.

Optimizing Your Final Cut Pro System
0-321-26871-7

The ultimate guide for installing, configuring, optimizing, and trouble-shooting Final Cut Pro in real-world post-production environments.

Final Cut Pro for Avid Editors, Third Edition
0-321-51539-0

This comprehensive "translation course" is designed for professional video and film editors who already know their way around Avid nonlinear systems.

Final Cut Pro 6 for News and Sports Quick-Reference Guide
0-321-51423-8

This easy look-up guide provides essential techniques for broadcast studios using Final Cut Pro to edit news and sports.

Shake 4 Quick Reference Guide
0-321-38246-3

This compact reference guide to Apple's leading compositing software offers a concise explana-tion of the Shake interface, workspace, and tools.

Compressor 3 Quick- Reference Guide
0-321-51422-X

Learn essential techniques for audio and video compression, batch-encoding, test-clip workflows, exporting podcasts, and more.

QuickTime Pro Quick-Reference Guide
0-321-44248-2

An invaluable guide to capturing, encoding, editing, streaming, and exporting media.

Final Cut Server Quick-Reference Guide
0-321-51024-0

Final Cut Server delivers intuitive media asset management, review and approval tools, and workflow automation.

Xsan Quick-Reference Guide, Second Edition
0-321-43232-0

Apple's exciting new enterprise-class file system offers high-speed access to centralized shared data.

The Apple Training Series

Apple Training Series: Mac OS X Support Essentials, Second Edition
0-321-48981-0

Apple Training Series: Mac OS X Server Essentials, Second Edition
0-321-49660-4

Apple Training Series: Desktop and Portable Systems, Third Edition
0-321-33546-5

Apple Training Series: Mac OS X Deployment v10.5
0-321-50268-X

Apple Training Series: Mac OS X Directory Services v10.5
0-321-50973-0

Apple Training Series: Mac OS X Advanced System Administration v10.5
0-321-56314-X

Apple Training Series: iLife '08
0-321-50190-X

Apple Training Series: iWork '08
0-321-50185-3